Coming
Full Circle

A Journey to the Edge of
Life and Back

SUZANNE RUGGLES

BALBOA.PRESS
A DIVISION OF HAY HOUSE

Balboa Press books may be ordered through booksellers or by contacting:

Balboa Press
A Division of Hay House
1663 Liberty Drive
Bloomington, IN 47403
www.balboapress.co.uk
1 (877) 407-4847

Because of the dynamic nature of the Internet, any web addresses or links contained in this book may have changed since publication and may no longer be valid. The views expressed in this work are solely those of the author and do not necessarily reflect the views of the publisher, and the publisher hereby disclaims any responsibility for them.

The author of this book does not dispense medical advice or prescribe the use of any technique as a form of treatment for physical, emotional, or medical problems without the advice of a physician, either directly or indirectly. The intent of the author is only to offer information of a general nature to help you in your quest for emotional and spiritual well-being. In the event you use any of the information in this book for yourself, which is your constitutional right, the author and the publisher assume no responsibility for your actions.

Any people depicted in stock imagery provided by Getty Images are models, and such images are being used for illustrative purposes only.
Certain stock imagery © Getty Images.

Print information available on the last page.

ISBN: 978-1-9822-8107-6 (sc)
ISBN: 978-1-9822-8105-2 (hc)
ISBN: 978-1-9822-8106-9 (e)

Library of Congress Control Number: 2019919368

Balboa Press rev. date: 12/02/2019

We shall not cease from exploration, and the end of all our exploring will be to arrive where we started and know the place for the first time.
—T. S. Eliot (1888–1965)

This book is dedicated to my incredible family and friends, and to my very special colleagues at Full Circle. I am blessed to walk beside you all.

For the Children – let them lead the way

CONTENTS

ABOUT THE AUTHOR

At age 6, Suzanne had a vision of the Himalayas and of silver birch trees in autumn. As this vision unfolded in a way that her young mind could understand, she was shown that life was like a road with many junctions. She was guided, in precise detail, to understand this was a route towards another perfect reality. She was shown that challenges, when viewed from different perspectives – such as junctions or crossroads – are simply moments in which to pause and consider, ultimately giving us opportunities to choose our direction. At these junctions, and through the choices we make, we are able to navigate our soul's journey.

In her twenties, Suzanne was a celebrated designer, featured as one of the top ten designers in London, Paris, and Milan. Her clients included Hollywood actors, ambassadors, royalty, and celebrities. At the height of her success, she was diagnosed with SLE (also known as lupus), a potentially life-threatening autoimmune illness. She eventually realised that this diagnosis was an opportunity to grow, so she embarked on a journey to find the best ways to manage her life with an incurable condition.

Years later her life was under threat again, this time when she contracted bacterial meningitis. She drew on all her knowledge and skills as she fought to survive, but as her condition worsened and the deadly infection took over her brain, she lost all control over her body. She left her body and floated towards the ceiling, held in a suspended state between life and death. Literally powerless to return, she realised the more she fought to hang on, the further away she seemed to drift away. At the moment she let go – ready to die – she received an extraordinary sign from above, a gift that would bring her back to life and bring her full circle.

This is a powerful, true story of a near-death experience. It describes how life's challenges, when viewed from a different perspective, can guide us back to our soul's purpose.

FOREWORD

It is usually only in hindsight that one recognizes the hand of the divine in shaping our lives. I now know that my meeting with Suzie and Full Circle Fund Therapies was one of the reasons I moved to the UK. Suzie had started the charity at the same hospital where I was working, Our vision was the same- to create a healing environment where we could offer patients Integrative therapies we believed would help in healing.

My first meeting with Suzie was in January 2014, a few months after my relocation to London from the USA. We were settled in the USA for close to twenty years, with a staff position at Mayo Clinic, where I practiced Integrative Medicine.

A job opportunity allowing us be closer to our parents lay ahead. The uncertainty and fear of the future lurked, yet we knew it was the right thing to do, with our elderly parents there, and a chance to bring our children closer to their extended families. In fact, I visited my spiritual teacher in India and prayed deeply for an answer as I could not decide if the move was the right thing for us. On my return to the UK from India, a few days before I returned to the USA, I received a call from the CEO of St. George's Hospital in London to hear that a job in Integrative Medicine would be created within the NHS (National Health Service), something unheard of in the UK. I knew I had to move to London.

After many meetings in the coffee shop, one day I asked Suzie her story.

What unfolded was profound, and with goosebumps and a knowing, I suggested to Suzie that she write her story. "Do you think people will believe me?' I recall Suzie's words... The name Full Circle had intrigued

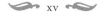

me, it was a name I was familiar with. As my spiritual master, Sathya Sai Baba said, *'Scientists put their faith in machines. The spiritual seekers place their faith in Mantras (spiritual chants). One is a scientist, the other is a saint. The saint believes in fullness. The scientist is content with half the circle. Spirituality represents the full circle.'* I shared my thoughts with Suzie on the name of the charity.

Full Circle Fund Therapies, represents Spirituality in Healthcare, a place where true healing occurs, a place offering evidence based integrated therapies, and staff caring for and serving patients...selflessly. Suzie's commitment and passion to her vision is difficult to describe. She works with a knowing, a gentleness, and great love with whoever she encounters to fulfil her work. What has developed is a friendship beyond a work encounter.

What you are about to read may change your belief about health, the spiritual dimensions that exist in our wellbeing, our meaning and purpose on planet earth, and so much more. Be open to the possibilities of life, the synchronicities, and let health and healing occur for each one of us on this planet.

Thank you for the opportunity Suzie. May many people's healing occur by sharing your story.

Dr Kavita Prasad BSc (Hons) MBBS FACP

PROLOGUE

Out of Nowhere

I don't know if you're calling me home, or if I am staying, I found myself saying in the darkness of my hospital room, my head pounding to the point it felt like it was breaking open, my temperature and fear levels rising out of control. But I continued with a strong sense that I had to add: *If I've got any say in the matter and, I beg you, please, let me stay; there are so many things I need to do, to finish.*

Part of me knew the grave danger I was in. That part of me knew I had to ask for help as every cell in my body was screaming with fear and pain. I had to ask for the biggest favour of my life. I thought, *If I'm being called home, please help me, as I am so, so scared of dying. I don't know how to die; I'm so afraid.*

I felt powerless in the enormity of what I was asking for. It was as if I was standing in complete darkness, peering over the edge of a skyscraper-tall cliff, my toes already over the edge. I couldn't move back. I knew then it was only a matter of time that I could remain here. I knew I wasn't brave enough to just step off into the thick darkness stretching out ahead of me. I felt certain it was only a matter of time before I fell or lost my balance or, what seemed even worse, that I had to physically choose to step off the edge. I knew I wouldn't do that willingly.

In that moment, as I asked for help for all I was worth, for the briefest of seconds I discovered I was in a glade of absolute light, and with it came a brief moment of clarity. I suddenly had the feeling that if I had to choose to step off the cliff, then that must mean I had a possible choice to stay. Right? Maybe? Possibly? I couldn't lose time thinking this through without letting more time slip from my grasp. I followed a pencil-thin line of clarity that seemed to indicate I had a choice.

I noticed at this moment that my mind had, for a brief moment, shifted gear and found its way completely out of my conscious control, into neutral. I was momentarily free from all superfluous thoughts, my unending hallucinations driven by the mental gunfire and rocket launchers going off in my head; my survival flailing thoughts of *what ifs* and *how can I survive?*; *will I have brain damage?;* to the unavoidable realisation that I was dying. In no way did I feel I was ready to cope with any of this. Whether I liked it or not I was on a juggernaut and was careering out of control.

My increasingly frantic thoughts were suddenly silenced. My mind screeched to a halt. I was in a momentary ceasefire. The pain in my head did not – or could not – abate, but surprisingly, with my mind now in neutral and without any conscious control on my part, my thoughts were able to trail off and became firmly focused on my work. To my surprise, I found myself in the corridor where I worked, a specialist bone marrow transplant unit which treats patients with leukaemia and other life-threatening blood disorders. I was aware I was hovering about halfway up the corridor – at about eye level. The corridor was fully lit and I was hovering outside each of the rooms of the patients I'd told I'd see tomorrow. This was my beloved project, for which I had had big plans, but because of the range of complexities setting up an innovative project, as this one was, in any hospital, was still in its infancy. I was busy scything my way through what seemed like acres of red tape and protocol. I was still laying the foundations. I was seeing great support for my project from nurses and physiotherapists, who were essential to its success, but I understood that it would take a while longer for the majority of our medical teams to really understand the value of my project for their patients. I had always understood what I had to do, and all this was wrapped up in a big ribbon that I hadn't even yet located – sustainable funding. As I saw it now, I was still miles from creating the blueprint to let people know how to carry it forward if I was gone. I hadn't factored that at all in to my plans before.

'You see?' I continued, tears rolling down my cheeks, my heart actually hurting with a heaviness and inconsolable sadness, 'I haven't finished yet ...'

CHAPTER 1

Splosh

We all hold a piece of the jigsaw but none of us can see the
whole image. We need each other to complete the picture.
—Christopher Cooke

E arlier that week, an odd thing happened. It was a cold January
day, and a clear blue sky crowned the Victorian buildings opposite
the cafe where I was enjoying lunch with some friends. The pale yellow
sun flooded through the windows. Outside, people scurried to and fro,
heads bowed against the cold winter air.

Out of nowhere, inside my head I experienced a splosh of fluid. It
entered the inner cavity of my right ear and seemed to fill it up, blocking
my hearing. I wasn't particularly alarmed, as I didn't have any pain or
discomfort. I just wondered what it could be and what was actually
producing the fluid. It felt similar to going underwater, combined with
how it feels when descending in an aeroplane. I didn't realise it then, but
time was now ticking towards a deadly outcome. A cocktail of bacteria
were now able to travel backwards and forwards, unchecked across what
is normally the semipermeable yet highly selective blood-brain barrier,
in place to protect the brain from any molecules or microbes which
could cause infection or damage.

I went to bed as usual that night. When I woke in the morning,
I had a terrible headache. This was accompanied by high-pitched

squealing noises coming from my right ear. My eardrum had burst in the night, and fluid had trickled down the side of my face and my jaw and onto my pillow. I went to the GP that morning, and she looked in my ear and concluded I had a very bad infection. I explained the fluid came from *within* my head, describing the large dump of fluid that had pooled inside my ear. Of course, my doctor said any large amount of fluid simply wasn't possible. The blood-brain barrier is made up of tightly crammed cells which form an almost watertight seal, letting only very specific tiny molecules and some gases to pass. The blood-brain barrier is the brain's tightly patrolled and highly organised armoury of defence, and for good reason. Simply put, it does not let the amount of fluid that I had just experienced pass through the barrier. Therefore, the GP was certain that it was a case of a bad ear infection. My doctor gave me antibiotics, prescribing the highest dose possible for safe measures. Feeling pretty groggy, I went back home to try to sleep off whatever was wrong with me.

By mid-afternoon I had faint hallucinations when I closed my eyes. My headache was getting worse, and my temperature had started to rise. I began to feel sick. I called the GP surgery for the second time that day. It was cold and dark outside as I sat huddled, ashen white, in the corner of the doctor's waiting room, my head in my hands against my advancing headache and increasing nausea. The GP prescribed anti-sickness medication, with instructions to contact the hospital if I still felt sick after a few hours.

I gingerly made it home; the pressure in my head caused a bone-splintering sensation across my forehead with each step. It was as much as I could do to get up the stairs and crawl straight into bed. I was sure the antibiotics and the anti-sickness medication would soon kick in. I tried to sleep but couldn't. My temperature had now climbed to more than forty degrees. My fiancé, Jean-Cyrille, called my parents. My mother called her GP, who immediately said, 'It sounds like meningitis. Tell your daughter she needs to get to A & E immediately'.

Jean conveyed this news to me. It was a shock! *Oh no*! I thought. *No, it can't be meningitis*. I feebly protested, with all the strength I could muster. I was certain there was absolutely no way I could manage to get to hospital. At this point I couldn't sit up, let alone stand up, as the pressure in my head had reached a screaming pitch.

I snapped at him. 'I can't get to hospital. I can't stand the light! I definitely can't hack A & E for a minute, let alone hours. I just can't bloody do it! I just can't. I just can't ...' My words trailed off, and I sobbed uncontrollably.

Jean-Cyrille tried his best to calm me, but an overwhelming sense of panic controlled my thoughts. Accompanying that was a fairly large dose of fear and not a little denial clouding my mind. I was in a strange void and was hardly able to face the enormity of what was ahead of me.

Every word caused my forehead to feel like it was being crushed. It was a pain I had never experienced. It felt as if my head was in a vice and was slowly being ratcheted tighter every hour. To complicate matters further, each sound or movement I made caused a reverberating pain, like a high-velocity pinball smashing into my skull.

I have to sleep, I kept thinking. It was all I could do now, but just as I was drifting off, a thought suddenly popped into my mind: I had to make a call to my work! I ignored that. *Outright ridiculous*, I protested to myself. I just wanted to bloody well sleep. I *had* to sleep; I *needed* to sleep.

Sleep is now climbing all over me—
A thick sea fog, an unknown shoreline.
I can't see clearly – unsteady in this terrain.
The sea fog shrouds me, depositing tiny droplets,
My forehead undimming the internal jackhammer.
My eyelids are drawn down by unseen gravity.
Gravity, I think. *That's funny*. The situation is grave.
And then it takes over again.
My eyes, I think, *I need to keep them open.*
Another thought rushes past itself: *I need to sleep.*
I will recover if I sleep. I am torn.
I blink intensely, trying to push back the friendless fog.
It accumulates more, asserting itself over me.
I push back again.
My mind is weary.
Stray papers by an open window,

Pinned under a grey stone.
It gathers once more, stronger against me now.
Sleep insists. I am weakening.
Thickening the air around me, it speaks to my lungs, to my eyelids.
Sleep.
Eroding my shoreline, pebble by pebble.
Eventually,
I begin to slip under, velvet sleep the promise.
A breezeless night,
My mind no longer a turbine.
Unplugged and fading,
My eyelids now gently, softly
Clamp shut.

CHAPTER 2

I Need to Ask for Your Help

Realize that everything connects to everything else
-Leonardo da Vinci

From under the heavy folds of sleep a clear thought suddenly burst into my mind. It jolted me awake with an imperative force that had an altogether different, piercing quality about it. It somehow bypassed my rapidly diminishing faculties allowing my mind to gain immediate traction on what I needed to do. . The message was absolute: *call the ward now* – not call someone, not call for an ambulance. Although I should already have known to do that, I didn't realise what was happening until I started losing mental function. No, the instruction which appeared into my mind arrived without any room for doubt. It was explicit. I knew in an instant what it meant. It meant call the ward where I was currently working. I didn't know it at the time, but this call would save my life.

It was now nearly nine o'clock at night. To my surprise and relief, a ward doctor answered the phone. She had only recently joined the medical team on the haematology unit but had already impressed me and my many clinical and nursing colleagues with her diligence, competency, and focus. Although at the time she would have been a relatively inexperienced junior doctor, she seemed to have 100 per cent focus on all her tasks. She also possessed something less tangible. I later recalled a conversation with one of the leading haematology consultants about her, and he said she was one of the best junior doctors he had ever worked with because, as he recounted, she had a natural instinct for discovering what was wrong. As the haematology unit's busy junior doctor, she often worked long hours to complete her workload. Even so, I remember being surprised that she was still there and had answered the phone that night. I was more than a little relieved that she happened to be there just at that moment.

It was so painful to speak because of the intense pressure in my head, which must have been pressing on a nerve, as my face felt sore from my forehead to my jaw. I dreaded having to speak and imagined recounting my symptoms with whomever picked up the haematology ward phone, hoping he or she would have the time to try to locate the on-call doctor. If left to my own devices, I would never have called the ward so late in the evening. I certainly didn't want to disturb them, as I knew how busy they were. It all felt as if it was in the "too-hard box".

However, my brain's insistent message to call the ward cut through all my worries and perceived difficulties. For some reason, I just acted without any further thought or questioning. I didn't think of it as an act of faith, but in a way I suppose it was. I recognised the quality of the message as being authentic and therefore worth acting upon. I realised this type of impelling thought doesn't happen often, especially with the clarity of this message. I understood it was important to make the call.

I vaguely mumbled my symptoms to the ward doctor, mainly about being increasingly sick and having this excruciating pain in my head. Really, I was hoping to simply seek her reassurance that I'd be fine – maybe she would suggest it was probably a migraine; that I should just rest; and it would be OK in the morning. Something like that would have been fine. Part of me, I thought, was a bit annoyed at having been woken up. I was already asleep and at least out of pain. *Sleep*, I thought – *that's exactly what I intend to do right after I finish this call.*

The young doctor listened patiently to my symptoms and my attempts to play them down. She saw through my overwhelming need to go right back to sleep.

Instead, she calmly said, 'Can you get to Accident and Emergency now, Suzie?'

Oh no! I thought. *No, I wasn't wanting her to say that. To go* to Accident and Emergency wasn't at all what I had planned to hear.

I protested. I trotted out reason after reason, but namely that it was impossible and especially so as I definitely couldn't cope with any lights. I was panicking at how I could even begin to manage A&E, let alone get down the stairs because the pressure was now too great in my head. Surely, I pleaded, didn't she think that with just a little bit of sleep I'd feel better in the morning?

She repeated gently but firmly, 'I need you to get to A&E now, Suzie'.

Anticipating, and perhaps having empathy for me, especially given my tearful pleadings at what seemed to me an almost impossible task ahead, she simply added, 'I'll find you a side room in A&E the moment you arrive. I promise you that, Suzie. I will meet you in A&E in ten minutes, and I'll have it all arranged so that I can take you straight through to a darkened side room'.

She added, 'I'm going down right now to get a room set up for you." She told me later she felt she was pretty sure she knew what she was dealing with and that, if she was right, left to my own devices, I would not have made it through the night.

Before hanging up, she said, 'Please promise me you'll leave now. I'll see you in ten minutes, OK?'

The calm urgency in her voice reached me; I suddenly understood I was running out of options, and sleeping it off was no longer one of them. It took me at least five minutes to get down the stairs; each step caused a greater build-up of pressure in my head than the previous one.

I was in a terrible place now. I thought my head quite literally would split open. Jean-Cyrille, bless him, held my hand as I descended each painful step. I gripped the banister with my other hand and negotiated with my terrified mind and body, imploring it to stay with me whilst I navigated each awful step to the ground floor. I had only one thing in my mind now, and that was to get to hospital.

Trying to get into the car was yet another challenge. Who knew the different air pressures that exist between a simple matter of getting down to street level and getting into a car?

Jean-Cyrille must have been extremely stressed, but he calmly managed to get me to hospital. When we got near, I remember him flouting the road signs which instructed cars to go around the hospital perimeter, because he knew this would have meant another five minutes or so. There were road humps around that perimeter road, which for any other reason around a hospital is a great idea, of course, but not today, he reasoned. Instead, calculating the risk, he drove the wrong way up the exit road meant only for ambulances, reasoning this was the quickest route to deposit me right outside the A&E front door.

It was freezing outside that night, and as I shuffled in I was shivering. By now, my light sensitivity was worsening. Just walking with my eyes three-quarters closed and my head enshrouded by my coat, the bright fluorescent lights of the busy emergency department found gaps in my fabric armour; the light seemed to lock on to a space behind my eyes, as if nerve-piercing spikes plunged straight through my skull into the depths of my brain. Because of this I needed my big black winter coat over my head rather than over my body. I pulled it closer, and closed my eyes.

True to her word, by the time I arrived, the ward doctor had already found a side room for me. She guided me in. As soon as she examined me, she noticed tiny red dots on my legs and on my stomach; the devastating tell-tale signs that septicaemia (sepsis, a potentially life-threatening infection) had already taken hold. She was in no doubt; I had meningitis and evidently blood poisoning too. If she was right, there was no time to do a lumbar puncture to know precisely what type of bacteria we were dealing with, and then to select the most appropriate antibiotic targeted for that particular strain. No. I was out of time for analysis.

Without hesitation, she knew what she had to do. Inserting a cannula into my arm, she hooked me up to two different types of antibiotics. It was the only option. I had almost no time left. Maybe I had reached or already passed the tipping point. It was her first and last-ditch attempt to find an antibiotic capable of stopping the rapidly proliferating toxins that already had a lethal head start and were busy colonising large swathes of the lining of my brain and spinal cord. She later told me that if I had arrived one hour later, it would have been too late to save me.

At about midnight I was transferred to another ward, where a darkened side room had been made available for me. This was effectively a holding ward whilst my results continued coming in through the night, giving a vital steer to my doctors of my bloodstream's contents, how my organs were holding up, and providing my medical team with a fast-changing microbiological landscape upon which decisions needed to be made.

As I lay there alone in this unfamiliar space, two drips constantly on the go through the night, I suddenly understood without a shadow of a doubt that I was more likely to die than live. Realising this, it felt as if I stopped breathing, caught in a weightless vacuum, not knowing what the next step would be. The full catastrophe now slowly percolated through my conscious thoughts. As I contemplated that this was likely the end, I suddenly felt inconsolably sad.

The pain in my head continued spiralling out of control in jagged peaks of intensity. I could hardly think because of this wrecking ball now occupying my head. Then, somehow, through the pain, another pain emerged, but it was different – it was an emotional, heavy pain that felt like it was pulling down on my heart. I was so sad to be leaving this life, to be leaving my family and friends, and to be leaving my project in the very hospital where I now was fighting for my life – my project, I protested loudly to no one in particular, is not finished.

Here I was, my project about to die with me, or at least be a much-reduced version of the one I had envisioned as I hadn't passed on any of it to anyone. I became acutely aware and frustrated that I hadn't had long enough to cut through all the red tape and put all the components in place yet. In response to my thoughts, my heart suddenly felt weighted down more, as if a boulder was pressing down, all life being squeezed out of me. This feeling made itself known: I was out of time. As this realisation dawned on me, I felt utterly inconsolable. This feeling rushed through me and brought with it a powerful mixture of anger and sadness, and the sheer enormity and equal and opposite futility of my situation now. I was acutely aware of the damage being caused to my brain with every second and every minute that had already passed.

I had been thinking about three of my patients in particular who, just before I'd been taken ill, I'd said to each one that I would 'see you tomorrow'. Tomorrow never came. Already a few days had past. It was always incredibly important to me not to break the fragility of hope when someone is fighting for their life. In all the chaos of the last few days, I suddenly realised I hadn't got a message to them. I hoped that one of my nursing colleagues had told them I had been taken ill so that they understood that was the reason I'd not been able to come back as I had promised.

I couldn't bear to focus on the reality; I was dying. As I thought about my project and all the plans I'd had for it, the next thing I received was a feeling that compelled me to 'explain' – I think is the only way I could describe it – as to why I wanted to live. I suddenly had a very real sense that I needed to *engage* my thoughts and explain *why* I wanted to live and why I wanted to live for *this* project. In thinking about this after the event, I often say it was a bit like presenting a business case with everything at stake.

I thought through the aspects, vision, and rationale for the project I had started just a few years previously on the haematology and bone marrow transplant unit, in the same hospital; in fact, my project was started on the ward right opposite where I was now lying. I suddenly became aware that my mind had become free, as if physically detached. I found that I was gliding down the ward, effortlessly propelled. What I was seeing was as if I was fully there somehow, as if I was tagging along on the coattails of my thoughts. I observed this new phenomenon with a mixture of fascination and incredulity. I noticed the corridor lights were on; I heard the buzzers were on and then switched off, as patients requested help for various reasons and the nurses hurried about to attend to them. What was interesting was in this time and space, my extreme light sensitivity, which was a serious feature of my physical condition at the time, such that I couldn't tolerate anything but a darkened room, was not a problem. It certainly wasn't a case of my thoughts being able to generate any of these images of the activity going on round the ward. No, absolutely not. I didn't have any energy for that.

I watched nurses coming and going, but I realised they didn't seem to notice me. I was hovering at about head height, so at first I didn't realise I didn't have my body there. Next, I realised I was outside and looking one by one at each of my three patients' doors. It was as if I was staring at the doors, pointing with my eyes and mind, thinking about each of them and the reasons they were there and how they had been suffering; two of them had blood cancer and one had catastrophic bone marrow failure, saying, 'You see? This is why'.

Just behind an isolation room door was a young mother who I'd said I would come back to see "tomorrow". She was admitted to our ward almost a year previously and had not been able to go home due to a devastating illness where her body didn't produce an immune system. She was just 19 years old, and for her, even the common cold could be fatal for her. She had been parted from her baby ever since her diagnosis. All the medication had sadly failed to get her immune system to generate. She had recently had her "last-hope treatment", which was a bone marrow transplant, and still her immune system failed to generate. Despite the grave nature of her illness and prognosis if her immune system continued to fail, her medical team, her nurses, and I were all stunned by her ability to remain positive in the face of mounting uncertainty.

'She's made of something special, that young lady', said one of the senior nurses. I agreed with him.

I knew her well, as we had had lots of chats in the last year whilst she was cooped up in her isolation room. Whatever seemed to happen to her, she always did the best she could to find something positive to hang on to that would help her face yet another setback that would scythe through her hopes of seeing her baby daughter again. I thought about her and people like her, who were enduring such hardship and at such a young age. I admired her grace and her quiet, galvanised determination and courage to take each minute at a time.

I was thinking too of all the work that I needed to do for the continuation of the project at the hospital, and suddenly, my mind lifted to an expansion of the project. As if in an instant it seemed to take in the whole of the country, including Scotland. In an instant, I was able to convey with my thoughts what I needed to do, and what I could set up if I had – or was given – more time.

I continued, my reality suddenly freighted in my mind: *I don't know if you're calling me home or if I've got a say in the matter, but if I have a choice, this is what I want to finish. I have to finish setting this up.*

I continued: *If, however, you are calling me home how can I resist you? But –* I added: *If.* I paused and thought deeply about what I was going to say next. *If I've got a say in the matter I beg you please let me live. I need to finish setting up this project.*

All the while I said this, I was still staring at the patients' doors and thinking of them. I thought of the operational project I already set up on the ward, which I knew was still too far off from what I wanted and believed was needed. I was thinking too about the much wider need throughout the country and how, if I set it up, it would help other likeminded souls, like nurses and doctors in other hospitals take the blueprint of what I had in my mind, so that it could be taken up by nurses (I always imagined nurses being central to this) and rolled out wherever they were. So long as they wanted it for their patients, it could be set up.

At some point shortly after my request was fully expressed, I found I was returned back into my current darkened room where the pain in my head raged undiminished. I now added a caveat to my request to stay. I had to. I was totally on the limits of my human ability to cope with the pain currently crushing my brain; I didn't know how much longer I had to live. Dying felt right then, as I was forced to contemplate it, like I would need to take a step off a precipice into the dark, not knowing what lay hundreds of feet at the bottom of the cliff.

I'm not ashamed to say it, but I wasn't brave enough to step off that cliff edge into the darkness. *If,* I continued, *you let me stay, I beg you please help me, because this pain is horrific and I don't know if, or how, I can cope with it much more; please help me.*

But if you're calling me home, well, I know full well I can't resist you, can I? But if this is what is going to happen, and I have no other options left but to die, please help me. I don't know how to die. I am absolutely terrified.

The moment I finished, an extraordinary thing happened. At that moment of my asking, I received an overwhelming sense that my request was heard. Almost as if in a reply, a "waterfall" of light (for I can only describe it as that) flowed through me. It swept in through the top of my head and effortlessly but absolutely perceptibly cascaded down through my body, bringing with it in one single, timeless moment a profound message of calm and an exquisite feeling of light. It is impossible to find words to describe it, but the closest I can think of is holding the lightest, sugar-fine sand, and letting it flow through your fingers. That perceptible feeling of lightness flowing through me was so infused with light, it brought with it an almost dancing, joyous energy. This is the closest I can get to describing what it felt like. It brought the deepest sense of peace I have ever known and an indescribable feeling of pure, clear, unconditional love.

In this new and absolute port of calmness that I now found myself in, I got a clear message which has stayed with me as vibrantly as it did that night: I understood that whatever name we call to, whether it is God, the Universe, All-that-is, Allah, or Life Force, the message was clear, that the 'name' itself we give isn't what is important. What is important is that you periscope your intention to a *belief* in a benevolent higher guiding force and crucially, it was made clear to me, *that you need to ask* for help. Those two things – that you believe or, for people who may struggle with believing, that they have the *intention* of believing that there is a higher benevolent, guiding force regardless of the name and that you ask for help

I also became aware that every part of me had now become unfathomably peaceful. I still didn't know if I was going to live or die, but it didn't seem to matter in this precise moment. Whatever was going to happen to me now, whether I survived or not, I was absolutely certain that what I had just experienced was divine and whatever route lay ahead – life or death – that I was being heard and therefore everything would be fine. I have no idea what time it was, but in the early hours of Friday, 17 January 2003, my life changed forever.

On a physical level, my pain continued to escalate uncontrollably, but what now became particularly evident was that each time I reached the absolute breaking point with the pain and my skull felt that it was breaking open, then, and without any effort or intervention on my behalf another, waterfall of light-love-peace flowed through me. Each crescendo of screaming, splitting, skull-crushing pain was followed by this waterfall infused with light and unconditional love. Each time it happened, I was brought back to an impossible place – by logical or scientific standards – of complete calm and a deep, peace-filled stillness. What was also extraordinary was that this rhythmic roller coaster of pain to the deepest state of stillness continued without any control on my part, for the next fifteen hours. Following each wave, my mind, without any conscious input, would regain profound calm. All my superfluous, fear-driven, energy-draining thoughts just evaporated. I noticed in these moments that I wasn't struggling to survive. My inner topography saw me repeatedly clamber up sharp escarpments of pain, and slip and stumble until, hands bleeding, I could climb no more. It was in that moment that the wave would again come through me that I would find myself as if in a lush, verdant, sun-filled valley, soothing my torn hands in the cool mountain stream. Despite myself, I was continuously guided back to a state of peaceful being. I wasn't thinking, *What if?* or *How can I survive this?* and instead found myself for the first time in my entire life just "being", my mind and body cushioned by a feeling of absolute peace. This wasn't the first time that I had peered over the edge of the precipice with my health and wondered what the next days would bring, nor was it the first time that I had experienced an overwhelming sense of being part of, and belonging to, something far higher, far purer, and far more benevolent than I can ever imagine or begin to describe. The next hours and days would tell if my wish to live was possible.

CHAPTER 3

I Can't Find My Nose

'Can you point to your nose?' This would be a simple request on any other day, wouldn't it? However, try as I may, I simply couldn't find my nose. *Odd,* I thought. *Where has it gone? Silly me,* I thought. *I'm just not concentrating.* After all, I reasoned, trying not to get alarmed at what had just happened, or to put it correctly, not happened, there was a perfectly logical explanation after all: I'd had no sleep for a couple of days, and it had been a bit of a trying few days. I was certain that was it.

Quietly commanding myself to concentrate, I tried again. I could see a sense of expectation in the eyes of the doctors surrounding my bed, I could see in their expressions they were willing me to locate and make contact with my nose. *I can do this,* I said to myself. *Come* on. *Focus.*

I poked and prodded again, certain this time of success. I knew, after all, where my nose was – it had been there quietly going about its business for the last thirty-eight years without my giving it much thought. This time I would make contact with my errant nose, and the looks of concern of those around me would dissolve.

I tried again. But no, it wasn't where it should have been. I stabbed my finger repeatedly into the front of my face where it certainly should have been. I widened my search, sweeping and prodding my finger in slightly different places, certain that I'd make contact any second now. But no. It was gone.

Not possible, I thought. A sense of panic took hold of me. Where the hell was my nose? Where *had* it gone? With rising alarm, I looked at the doctors, whose expressions had noticeably changed. I caught the eye of one of the young student doctors who was standing at the back of the assembled group of doctors. Because of the number of medical and nursing personnel crowding around my bed, this young doctor was just inside the door of my small room. Why did she look so worried? Was it sadness?

I couldn't tell, but I saw her expression change. I didn't want to think about what had just changed in her mind, so I darted my eyes back to the consultant standing to my right, a tall, kind-faced man. I studied his face for tell-tale signs of what he was thinking – what was his diagnosis? But he maintained a calm and kindly demeanour and continued doing a few other tests.

I felt the air in the small, overcrowded room become heavy. I could hardly breathe. The expressions of the others in the room slowly revealed to me what I feared. I was clinging to hope, and the consultant seemed calm. But in reality, my heart was already sinking. I tried once more, desperate to stop them from recording into my notes what I knew was about to happen. I was frightened of all the ramifications of what their assessment might mean.

I gave it one last attempt and restarted my futile prodding. *I can get this,* I urged myself. Again, no success. *No! No! No,* I screamed silently. *This can't bloody well be happening.*

Reading my increasing panic and to reassure me, the consultant gently said, 'Don't worry, your brain is under a lot of pressure right now; try to rest. Try not to worry for now, and we'll come back later'.

The rest of what he said was a blur. By this point the tension was unbearable. I desperately wanted the atmosphere to change. My life depended on something that was slipping from me. For some reason, I suddenly smiled broadly and blurted out, 'At least I'll make a perfect Picasso muse now!' Thankfully, we all laughed, changing the dense atmosphere for a brief moment.

They filed out of the room. I was left with my thoughts screaming at me in the silence. I felt my heart beating in my neck. I knew. They knew. I had just failed the test for brain damage.

My mind was racing at what this new twist would mean for me. Was this transitory? Was this permanent? What were my odds now? Even if I survived, did this mean I would be brain damaged? In my head I sounded just like I always did, but maybe – what if – I said things that were was as jumbled up as my actions were now? I suddenly had a creeping doubt that I was losing, little by little, to know where my edges were.

My thoughts trailed off. There was a knock at my door. It was my lovely friend and neighbour Anne. She must have heard from Jean-Cyrille earlier that morning and popped in to say hello before she went to work. She brought a lovely get-well card; it was a pretty painting of a garden titled "Garden Path in Spring". I saw it and felt a stabbing in my heart; I could hardly find my breath again. I didn't want to cry as I didn't know if I could ever stop.

Meanwhile, Anne was doing her best to be upbeat and cheery, and I wanted to stay with her on that waveband for as long as I could. I was so grateful to see her, to be near her gentle energy, her goodness. It was good to be reminded that there was a bustling world beyond my darkened room and outside my sentry guard walls. It was good to hear it was sunny outside that cold January morning. As a child, I always took a moment to drink in the cerulean sky when it graced us in the depths of winter. I always felt nature was such a gift to life, a chance to recollect; it always felt like a message to my young mind that seemed to communicate, *This winter too will pass, so stay strong, little one. There is a spring to come.*

CHAPTER 4

Silver Birch Trees in Autumn

The early seeds of my love of nature and its inherent beauty took hold at an early age. Our family home was set on its own land, nestled deep within the ancient wilderness of the New Forest in Hampshire. We moved there, my mother, Alison, father, John, and older sister, Karen, when my father moved jobs to Southampton. We moved there from Surrey when I was about 3. From as early as I can recall, I appreciated how our new house was orientated to nature. Not only was it built on top of a small hill to maximise the sense of space and light, but from every room you could see at least two big views of nature. In all directions, fields merged into thousands of acres of the ancient woodlands beyond. The New Forest seemed to stretch out endlessly, letting us in on its secrets for the precious moment in time that we were there and custodians of a piece of land in its midst. Long, hot summers gave way to biting, cold winters, so cold the pipes sometimes froze, and we would remain snowed in for weeks.

I learned to enjoy each season for what it gave: a vivid palette of life and colour. We were blessed to have such diversity of nature all around us. In the New Forest, little village communities sit embedded in nature and the landscape; wild ponies and cows roam free right outside your school gate; the call of the curlew's plaintiff cry across the heather-draped valleys, a busy little stonechat hopping from gorse bush to gorse bush acting as the sentry for all around. Two-hundred-year-old oak trees stood side by side with elegant beech trees, who were one of the first of the big trees to share their verdant young leaves each spring. At the back of our house were cherry trees which, many years before a thoughtful former owner had planted in a semicircle so that the tips of their bud laden branches formed a natural arch from one tree to the next. Every morning in spring before I went to school and when I returned home later that afternoon, I watched patiently for signs of the buds which in time would deliver a riotous arch of frothy blossom. On seeing this, I felt such joy as a young child, as it meant we were at last emerging from a long, harsh winter.

Whatever I was doing, I found I marvelled at the natural harmony all around. I noticed from an early age the patterns that seemed to emerge in what at first glance seemed a wilderness landscape – huddled fronds of last year's rust-coloured bracken looking downcast and unpromising were slowly reborn under the warmth of the late spring sunshine to unfurl into vibrant pea-green sculptural arcs, each frond perfectly adapted to thrive in the many shady and damp knells throughout the landscape.

My journey to school was through sandy marshlands which were alive with bird life, and the narrow country road meandered through a valley carpeted in aubergine-coloured heather. Clustered along the route were fearsome spikes of the native gorse whose deceptively fragranced yellow flowers smelt of coconut in high summer! On the far horizon, high ridges offered their statuesque sentries of pine trees up to the skyline. Closer to home, outside our gate, the forbidding clumps of gorse seemed to my young mind to stand guard over the ancient Roman burial mounds, which benevolently had long since given over their space to become a homely network of burrows for numerous families of rabbits.

From high up on the windswept heather-carpeted ridges, I loved to look below to see the little green fields studding the valleys, a green mosaic created by man's attempt to both tame and be sustained by nature in this majestic landscape.

To the front of our family home the drive came round a central teardrop-shaped lawn planted with a small group of silver birch trees. I loved the gracefulness of its leaf canopy particularly in full summer as it gave a delicate, dappled light, never a dense, cool shade like some of the other trees in the New Forest, but just enough to shield from the harshest summer sun. These indigenous silver birch trees of my childhood possessed rugged trunks which resembled a slightly scruffy camouflage paint job in shades of muddy white and soot-grey.

Early one summer morning, I came out of the house, past the lawn of these silver birch trees on my way to a fence which would take me across a small field and to the yard beyond, where we stabled our ponies. I remember being shorter than the top fence post, so getting under it and through the two strands of wire was very easy for me at that age! I was about 6 years old. I was about to climb through the fence when suddenly I saw a mountainous scene. I saw with clarity what appeared to be a steep mountainside with a woodland planted with hundreds of tall, slender trees with trunks of pure white. It seemed as if it must be autumn in this vision, as the leaves gave the scene a luminous shade of saffron, gold, and washed yellow. I was particularly drawn to the trunks of the trees in this vision. I somehow understood that these were silver birch trees, but they looked nothing like the silver birch trees I was used to, as they had the smoothest and whitest trunks I had ever seen. I was transfixed at the light too, which reached through the delicate leaves, and their golden colour mesmerised me. I knew to remember this scene; it was as if it was being seared into my memory. In my young mind, I simply accepted this vision, understanding the yellow-hued leaves crowning the milk-white trunks were birch trees in autumn. The colour pure white, and the yellow is a scene that has always stayed as vivid and as clear in my memory as if I saw it today. I find I am always looking for that image – perhaps in a painting, perhaps in a photograph.

As this scene was presented to me, what unfolded – for this is all I can describe it as – was being given a "package of pure knowing". It didn't contain any words, certainly not as we know words, but somehow the message arrived into my small person's consciousness as a fully formed, clear, and understandable message. It came somehow encoded so that I could understand it and accept it as, simply, a deep knowing. It felt as if the message that was conveyed to me was able to be immediately understood and assimilated directly into my mind and being. It was a message that came accompanied with the most expansive sense of peace, gentleness, and sense of limitless love, and the tenderest of care.

It is impossible to use mere words to explain a fraction of the feeling that it gave me or what it felt like, or what followed, as words are too constricted to convey the enormity of the feeling or the clarity and the ease with which I received its message. I became aware that I was being protected by something that had extraordinary benevolence and kindness. I use the "extraordinary" intentionally, even though it doesn't fully capture the feeling, but because it is closer to conveying the enormity or expansiveness, or even limitlessness that accompanied the feeling of benevolence and kindness that seemed to flow to me, around me, and through me. I was then made aware that some tough things would be coming my way in my life. I remember noting this, but strangely, I wasn't scared by this prospect, perhaps because I was still fully aware of the enormous benevolent feeling surrounding me, also I had no knowledge of what "tough things" could mean.

I suppose, like a child does, I simply accepted this part of the message and took it in stride. I felt like I was almost consciously and, at the same time, unconsciously suspended. All the while I was cushioned for a brief moment away from the outside world, as if in the lightest feather down duvet had somehow embraced me, and I was enveloped in an energy of the purest dancing light-infused loving care, and it was this lovely energy that brought me this message.

I recall being shown a road, as if I was floating above it and looking down on it. I was then made aware, as I looked at the road from above, that there were various junctions along that road. I was guided to focus on a junction point in the road. I realised I was focusing, as if I was almost hovering with my mind, over this particular junction, as if I was mentally paused. None of this was under my conscious control, and as I have said, it is impossible to use words to sufficiently convey what happened. What it felt like and what was communicated was all received simultaneously and within what I can only describe as a "whole package of knowing". I seemed to experience with all my senses and simultaneously understand what was being conveyed. Of course, all of it happened in an instant and in a nonverbal way.

The message continued, and I remained with the pause button on, so to speak, so that I presume my young mind would be able to focus and remember. As I continued to look at the junction point in the road, it was being revealed to me that the purpose of this image was that I would need to remember that I had a choice in life. It was delivered to me in such a way that I understood that through my life this image of the road and its junctions would be important. I understood too that the junctions were where I would have the opportunity to remember that I have a choice and that each choice would be bound up in the decisions I would make throughout my life.

When it felt as if the fullness of this part of the message – contained in the imagery of the road and the junctions was absorbed and calibrated within me – the message began to unfold again.

At this point, I was made aware that *this life is not the only life.* I was then shown how every decision that I would make, every action I would take, positively or negatively, had something similar to having points attached to each choice or each decision. It was then made clear to my young mind that these points are taken across to our next life; it was clear that *that* was the real destination and purpose. At this point, I was shown the most beautiful scene to the left of me: a magnificent and radiant scene of wide, green valley on a perfect summer's day. This message came with a clear, unwavering awareness despite my immature mind, that I understood it to mean that through the choices that I would make in this life, I would be able to move towards that beautiful destination in the next life.

Another interesting aspect of this vision is that I did not feel like I was a child receiving any part of this message. It wasn't given in any childlike manner; it seemed to assume and be transmitted on an ageless frequency. It seemed effortless, full of grace and with that, the entire beautiful message was gently sown into my awareness. What I have always marvelled at is how its delivery transcended my 6-year-old mind and comparatively limited scope and ability at that age to comprehend, let alone concentrate. Not only that, but for the message to endure with such clarity and in its entirety to this day is a marvel. It is, of course, impossible to find sufficient words to encapsulate a fraction of this whole experience or what it felt like, but this is the closest to the heart of it as I can articulate in words.

For many years, I never shared this with anyone, not for any reason other than I couldn't work out how to even begin to put into words the essence of the message. I also felt the message was sacred, although I didn't know the word or concept of that when I was young of course. It was a feeling. I just understood it was special and to be honoured, protected and treasured. I often wonder if I'll ever find the wooded mountainside that I saw in this vision.

I was changed by this vision and its message. It has been my quiet and constant compass through most of my life. At times I have so hopelessly and totally forgotten about it, so busy have I been in dashing here and there in the course of my hectic life, but something usually eventually triggers my mind to remember it, and I instantly latch on and let it be my guide again. At times of great personal challenge or when I was caught up in the freneticism of life or emotional reaction, I found that if I remembered its message of a bigger picture in life than we can imagine, it helped me return to that place of calm and soon after I would find I had arrived at a solution. In business, particularly having had this vision and understanding its message, it certainly meant I lost money in lots of ways, as you can't ever forget that you can't benefit from another's vulnerability – in business or in life. But even if it meant I lost money, somehow within me I felt that another day and maybe not even this life would provide the rebalance to my current loss. That, it has to be said, takes some doing, and I'm not sure I always got it right. But the point is, I always tried to weigh up the choice that presented itself when I was at a junction or a challenge, knowing often the choice in business caused me financial pain but somehow trusting in the message and what seemed to be its truth. Someday, I always thought to myself, it would all be ok.

To live like this in our fast-moving, commercially fixated world has been a constant challenge. There are times when I've been aware that it would be so much easier to forget it and throw myself fully into the waters of the way the world is. But before I dived in to the rough and tumble of that existence, something would tug at me and remind me of the reality. There have been times that I have forgotten about it altogether and then only realised a long time after an event, or remembered too late. I have always had an awareness that connecting to the frequency of the vision's energy is a bit like a muscle that I need to keep exercising to counteract the opposite heavier, and somehow easier, pull of day-to-day life. I continually strive to be mindful to reconnect to keep me in range of that exquisite energy that surrounded me when I was receiving the silver birch teaching.

When I felt tempted by the quick fix of commercial life, which is so abundant, I try to catch myself, to pause, to listen to and trust my ability to interpret the synchronicities that will come my way, to redirect me to the people or events I need for my soul to grow. Its message came to me in a myriad of ways, large and small, throughout life. When I was faced with a challenge, each time I noticed how, when I asked for guidance, I would be helped and somehow guided through. In the end it was a beautiful reminder of why we are here, and it was always more than enough for me.

CHAPTER 5

Let's See What Happens

'I shouldn't buy anything', the girl dressed in the smart, tailored business suit said to me. There was a sadness in her eyes. 'I have no idea if or when I'll get another job, but I feel I need to buy something from your gallery'. She paused. 'Being in this space and having an item from here, however small …'

Her words trailed off, as if she was in deep thought. 'I can't explain it logically. It somehow gives me hope to be in here, and I need to take a part of that feeling with me'.

This young lady told me she had just lost her job in the city an hour ago. It was August 1990. Iraq had invaded Kuwait the month before, and the city and global stock markets were in freefall. I was 25 years old and had just opened my first business in London's wonderful Fulham Road. My first gallery was special. And it became mine in an unusual way.

'We're off on a trip to Scotland', I announced to a friend who had just arrived from Australia via Stanford for a well-deserved holiday after finishing his PhD. I added, 'Oh, and I hope you don't mind, but on the way back I'd like to stop by a blacksmith!'

At the time, I had a great job working for one of the regional heads of Benetton UK. I had a wonderful and kind-hearted Italian boss who, from my very first day working for him, encouraged and guided me to progress through the business. In my spare time I studied business, finance, and law, and on weekends, I wrote lyrics and recorded songs. I wasn't looking to change direction. Life, it turned out, had other plans.

A few weeks earlier, I had picked up a magazine, and a beautiful black and white photograph of a chair caught my eye. Its back panel was a suspended circle of laurel leaves, the whole, an exquisite design fashioned out of wrought iron. Up to then I thought iron was for gates and railings or garden furniture. I was mesmerised by its intricacy, and equal and opposite to that, its strength. I was intrigued at how nature could be re-created in such a delicate and creative way, especially in such a tough material as iron. What seemed so clever to me as my eyes pored over the magazine's photograph was how it had now become an elegant, *useable* work of art. My mind was at once alive; it was as if a creative touch paper had been lit.

I contacted the blacksmith who had originally made this piece. He kindly offered to teach me how to construct and design in this tough material. I immediately made plans to go back to his forge, and when I did, I was shown some of the techniques for "smithing" so that, under the right circumstances, the stern, unbending material is made as pliable as children's Play-Doh. This transformation fascinated me. It was a revelation to discover how a material like this is able to be curved and moulded, split or twisted into the most complex and detailed shapes and can take the form of an airborne pen-and-ink drawing.

I returned from my visit with my mind full of design ideas. I'd loved art as a child, but I had no formal training in design. To my surprise, and as it turned out rather luckily, I discovered I could see my design ideas in 3D, and even more fortunate was when I drew them, I seemed to draw to scale. I did a few of what I thought were quick sketches of imagined chairs and sent them as a thank you to the blacksmith who had just taught me. I wasn't expecting a response. To my surprise he said, 'We love them and have started making them for you this morning!'

'That's fantastic', I said, 'but what we going to do with them ...?' I stuttered, 'I mean, where are we going to sell them?' I definitely hadn't formed a clear plan for that step yet.

He simply replied, 'You never know" mischievously adding, 'Let's see what happens!'

A few days later I got back to my office at Benetton, and I received a call. It was the husband of one of my work colleagues, and he knew about my new interest in designing furniture. In fact, he and his wife were my first clients for these early designs. He was working at the time for a marble company, and he told me they had just decided to look for someone to take over the lease of a showroom space that they owned.

He told me enthusiastically, 'It has two levels, the rent is very reasonable, and it's in Chelsea!' The rent was indeed very reasonable, but more than that, the property, I was soon to discover, was positioned in one of the most prestigious roads of London. *That is a stroke of luck!* I thought.

Number 90 Fulham Road was situated in an elegant parade of tall, beautifully proportioned buildings built in the late 1800s in a leafy area known as South Kensington. The area was home to some of the finest examples of white stucco fronted houses in London. These houses were first built in 1845 and were designed around beautifully planted garden squares. Early inhabitants included novelist William Makepeace Thackeray who, it is said, wrote *The Virginians* there, as well as Vice-Admiral Robert FitzRoy (1805–65), commander of HMS *Beagle*, on which Charles Darwin sailed.

Number 90 flanked these pristine, column-fronted residences. Walking into number 90, I knew it was special. Its lofty ceilings gave a cathedral quality to the space. Its tall windows faced south, and its marble floor, a platter of cool offset by a warm hue, was reminiscent of Jersey cream. Whatever was presented in this space always seemed to somehow become elevated in these surroundings.

On the road outside, London buses and taxis took eager passengers to the glitzy watering holes and shopping opportunities of Knightsbridge, which ran directly off from the top of Fulham Road. A stone's throw south, and running parallel to the Fulham Road, sat the King's Road, peppered with its quirky, independent-minded retailers, selling coffee to fashion to everything in between. Its quirky disciples strolled the pavements of the King's Road, reliving a vibe originally made famous in the 1960s when it was at the centre of a new era of expression and liberation in London.

A few months later I designed a collection, and it was all delivered to number 90. For quite a moment after the delivery lorry pulled away, I thought, *What on earth have I done?* It had been a whirlwind and a steep learning curve to have got to this point. Yet here I was at age 25 with a gallery which was now home to a new collection of furniture. This was the first of many times I would marvel at how a series of coincidences would take an idea and help me navigate options and possibilities to transform it into a reality.

Despite the turmoil and uncertainty in the world outside, number 90 remained vibrant, joyous, exciting, celebratory, and also a sanctuary. Shortly after opening, I was fortunate to be featured as one of the top ten designers in London, Paris, and Milan by a leading Japanese design magazine. Exciting private and commercial design commissions started flooding in, including a unique table design for the Victoria and Albert Museum's Friend's Room, and specially designed pieces for the Royal College of Music and the Birmingham Philharmonic Hall.

Some fascinating people walked through the doors of number 90 too, attracting ambassadors and artists alike. I was looking for new possibilities of what I could hang on the walls. I knew it needed to be original and complement the furniture around it.

A young photographer called David Scheinmann just happened to come by my gallery to enquire if I'd like to hang any of his work. He had not long finished his degree at Manchester University. I was interested as soon as I saw David's portfolio of work. I was excited by his originality. His quiet, unassuming persona belied the power of his creative ideas. His artistry really struck a chord in me; I had rarely seen photographs that had such an ethereal quality, and the techniques he used greatly inspired me.

A few days later he brought in about twelve exquisitely framed photographs, each piece a statement in its own right, either in scale or content. One, a powerful sepia image which hung over my desk, was more than five feet high and nearly four feet wide. One of the first pieces he unwrapped that day was from a photograph in a washed wood frame, the image originally one of his early commissions by the makeup company Rimmel. It was a beautiful photograph, but what was so ingenious was what he had done with the paper that the image was developed on to. David was an artist, and instead of using some form of photographic paper, he used handmade Chinese rice paper, edges frayed naturally. And then, during the process of developing the image himself, he had experimented with different chemicals, which either destroyed the image completely and the paper with it, or, as in the piece he just freed from its temporary shroud of bubble wrap, it gave the paper and its refined image a dramatic appearance, giving it texture and depth, reminiscent of 3D contours on a map. I was transfixed and didn't hesitate to give David a permanent exhibition.

Some of his work was of music icons of the time, so near my desk hung a dramatic composite photograph of musician Peter Gabriel, which sat alongside the album cover that he photographed for the band Tears for Fears. In another section of the gallery, we put a trio of photographs that David had been commissioned to take for one of the productions of *La Traviata* at the English National Opera. Shortly after we hung David's work at number 90, I noticed a man studiously observing David's work and in particular his images for *La Traviata*. He was interested to learn more, and I shared all that I could. He then introduced himself to me as the creative director of the Royal Ballet. From that first visit, he went on to commission David to photograph the prima ballerinas of the Royal Ballet at the world-famous Royal Opera House, in the heart of London's Covent Garden.

What I was trying to do most with my own designs and those of the photographers and artists that I chose to represent was showcase artists who embodied creativity, whether through colour or form or thought-provoking content. The work I selected encapsulated an essential connection that we have with each other and with nature.

'Never mix tulips with other flowers!' I recall a Danish flower artist saying to my astonishment one spring morning. 'They don't like sharing with other flowers; they die quicker'.

As if to answer my inquisitive look, she continued. 'Put them on their own. That way they'll be happy. They will perform – just *watch* as their stems arch and their shape changes!'

She had studied flower sculpture in Copenhagen before coming to live in London. She had walked into my gallery, and I was immediately inspired by her original design talent, her affinity with nature, and her knowledge of flowers.

In a response to the way this designer worked with living flowers, I designed a special collection of tall, eye-level vases to show off their precious contents. I found a talented glass artist who had a thriving glass studio on the south side of the River Thames in Battersea. He created for me translucent handblown glass vases which, in order to create texture, were often rolled in fine sand. They were among our best sellers, and on more than one occasion, from the moment they arrived into my gallery space to be unpacked, they were purchased by a client the moment flowers were put in! Their floral cargo changed with the seasons, from cerise pink paper-thin blossom on long arching stems in spring, to delicate fronds of cow parsley and hedgerow wildflowers picked in the fading light of a warm summer's evening, to bright firework flashes of oranges which belong to the exotic, bird-head-shaped strelitzia (bird of paradise) flower, bought from the flower market in the dark and misty light of a midwinter dawn. Each vase gave the observer, if they wanted, a moment to enjoy a palette of colour, or a delicate fragrance, or simply an opportunity to enjoy the architectural shapes found in nature. These glass vessels allowed me to reconnect to my innate need for reflection on the natural design abundant in nature. Whether picked from a rural hedgerow or plucked with precision from a far flung hothouse, the beauty and miracle is there if you look; each flower and petal is a design triumph of natural engineering and proof of symbiosis.

CHAPTER 6

All in a Day's Work

My gallery was never first and foremost about money. It was always other than that. It was about creating a space and designing pieces that somehow made the spirit soar and at the same time anchored the soul in the sustenance found for it in nature.

However, there was no escaping the material pressures of running a business when the costs of being in the heart of thriving Chelsea started to rise to unsustainable levels. So, I made the decision to relocate the business to a two thousand-square-foot former Victorian laundry known as the Old Imperial Laundry. It was conveniently located just across the River Thames in a vibrant area known as Battersea. The aim of this move was to build up my trade business and to focus more on working with architects and designing collections for exhibitions. The space was enormous, with thirty-foot-high ceilings and 150-year-old exposed beams, and the laundry's original glass roof lights lined either side of the roof's capacious apex. The high walls exposed the original Victorian handmade bricks, and to set off the furniture, we laid a stone floor, creating stone slab effects in the concrete before it set, and then applying layers of chalk paint to create a surprisingly believable handmade stone floor. The whole effect as clients entered through the original cathedral high wooden doors caused quite a sensation!

Commissions and orders started coming in from all over the world, including the United States, Japan, Australia, Italy, and Russia. It was at my first exhibition that an American lady came to talk to me about my designs. We sat on one of my sofas and chatted about all sorts of things, including the furniture, but rather amazingly, in such a short time, our conversation took us to talk about the synchronicities in life!

She said something a bit edgy, and I playfully tapped her on her left knee and said laughingly, 'You can't say that!' I was aware that people were watching us, but that's normal at an exhibition, so I thought nothing more of it.

After a while of chatting, she got up to leave and asked her assistant to give me his card. Their location was California.

A little while after she left, another artist came up to me and said, 'What was she like?'

Surprised by his question and trying to think who he could mean, I said, 'Who?'

He said, 'You know, who you were just talking to'.

Still baffled, I tried to think who he meant. As soon as one client leaves another comes up, so you don't really have time to think. I was stumped as to who he meant.

Putting me out of my misery, he said, 'You know – Cher'.

I looked at him incredulously, and exclaimed, 'No, that wasn't Cher. That was someone who looked like Cher, but no'. I thought back to her and my conversation. 'I'm sure it wasn't Cher!'

A moment passed. He looked at me and burst into laughter, adding, 'Oh yes, that was definitely Cher, everyone's buzzing that she came here and spent so much time with you. Everyone wants to know what you were speaking about'.

I had to laugh. If I had known it was her, I'm sure I would have acted differently. I guess for someone like Cher, who is under public gaze and scrutiny all the time, it was probably quite refreshing to be treated like a normal human being for once.

Later that autumn, I was showing at another exhibition in London and heard a buzz that Cher was coming. She came straight to where I was exhibiting and greeted me as if we were old friends, giving me a big hug and kissing me on both cheeks. We chatted effortlessly, this time swapping stories on a book we were both reading at the time – *The Road Less Travelled* by Scott Peck. I very much liked her spirit.

My knack of not recognising people happened a few times. At number 90, a tall, imposing man walked in. I guessed he was in his late fifties. He walked purposefully through the gallery space. I thought, without knowing who he was, *That man has an incredible air about him.* He just seemed to own the space in which he walked. He looked around and very quickly came to a decision on what his purchase was to be; it was a table. He paid, requested a specific delivery time of four o'clock the following afternoon. He gave his name: Alan Rickman. The next day, Guy, the delightful young man who did my deliveries, duly went to Notting Hill where Alan lived to make the delivery. When Guy came back, we had a little laugh. As planned, Guy was at the property precisely at four. The door opened, and ever the thespian, Alan was still in his pyjamas.

A while after, Guy told me he was soon to stop his delivery company as he planned to go to Hollywood, he said, to 'try my hand at making movies'.

I was more than a little surprised at his decision, but he gave me lots of notice and, also kindly, had found another delivery man who he recommended which, he didn't need to do, but this was very much Guy: very efficient, respectful and thoughtful. I was slightly worried for him that his dream, like so many others before him who headed to Hollywood, would end in let-down. I guessed the odds were stacked against him, but I was genuinely thrilled for him. I admired his get-up-and-go and willingness to follow his dream.

Funnily enough, a few years after he left, I was desperate to get something delivered, and because of how busy we were in the business, I urgently needed another pair of hands to help the following afternoon. Wondering if Guy had perhaps come back to the United Kingdom, I called the number I had on file for him and his mother answered.

I explained my predicament, and she gave me a number for him and said mischievously, 'Do call him, it will do him good!'

I did. It was late morning when I made the call, and I was a little surprised to find him sounding like I'd just woken him up. I apologised and asked if by any chance he was back in the UK, might he have a little time to help me.

He kindly replied, 'I'm actually still in the States, Suzie. I'm so sorry I can't help'.

After a few years in the Old Imperial Laundry, I found that I missed the buzz of being in Chelsea with a road frontage. By now, the trade side of my business was in full swing, but I was ready to have the best of both worlds and get back to the creativity and immediacy of designing and showcasing pieces for private clients.

The traffic was slow-moving in the King's Road one sunny spring afternoon. It was rush hour, and I happened to be caught in this part of the road. As I slowly edged my car forwards, looking forward to getting home, I noticed a 'For Lease' sign on an interesting building near the famous World's End section of the King's Road. The next morning I enquired and did the figures; they stacked up.

After some negotiation and a few months, I was in possession of the lease of five floors of an almost derelict building in the heart of London's King's Road, two doors up from legendary fashion designer Vivienne Westwood. As soon as I could, I had builders working on all floors to complete it in time for the launch date, which was set for July. I was committed to making this happen, so I was working all hours, ensuring orders were fulfilled and shipped all over the world. On top of this, I was busy designing a new collection, as well as curating the launch exhibition with a group of artists and sculptors. In addition to the time pressures, I was also project managing the building works to renovate each of the five floors out of their sad state, all with a tight deadline in time for the launch, invitations of which had already gone to the press.

Very quickly, I had tenants lined up for the top three floors so that rather neatly, as soon as possible paid the rental cost for the whole building. I was amazed no one had spotted this potential with the building before. Effectively, I had a rent-free space for my design business, which consisted of two glorious floors of south-facing, light-filled gallery space. What's more, I had built up a significant, loyal private and commercial client base established from number 90 and from the more recent base in the Imperial Laundry. In effect, I had tried to have as many bases covered financially as possible.

Now firmly back in the heart of Chelsea, I had a viable business and two floors of gallery space in one of the best "design" roads in London. The two levels were interconnected at the front by a newly painted white spiral staircase, attached to which I designed a floating triangle of transparent Perspex, the purpose to act as an "invisible" display shelf, which meant that any item in that window – whether a bright yellow recycled oil drum repurposed as a chair by French artist Olivier Vincent, or a sculpture in steel of a runner piercing through a sheet of steel – whatever was the chosen occupant that day appeared to *float in space, halfway up the tall glass window!* This shelf was meant to be just big enough to carry one design at a time; to be a celebration, be it a funky, eye-catching chair, a thought-provoking sculpture, or one of my specially designed handblown glass vases often full of willow branches and hedgerow flowers, brought back from the country after visits to my parents. I used to love watching the reactions of people busy daydreaming in the buses that filed slowly past the window on their way up and down the King's Road. As the buses' occupants casually gazed out of the windows, somnambulant in the slow-moving vehicles, their eyes suddenly alive by the surprising suspended firework of creation in the window. It always delighted me to see the wake up and then the double take!

By the end of June 1996, the builders were close to finishing the gallery space. The upper floors had already been completed and were immediately let out to friends. I offered them a rate that was extremely preferential for them but still, amazingly, covered pretty much the bottom line of my costs. The launch date had been set for mid-July, furniture, artwork, photography, and sculptures were already in storage waiting for the green light.

I had all my ducks neatly in a row. Here I was, right in the middle of the King's Road. I had the financial bottom line covered, and at last I felt I could fly with my design and curating ideas and concepts! I thought, *This is really going to be fun now!*

CHAPTER 7

Good News and Bad News

'I t's good news and bad news', my consultant said matter-of-factly. The week before, I had gone to my GP, as I had been having very sharp pains behind my eyes and blurred vision. I couldn't put my finger on what was wrong, but I just felt that something wasn't right. My GP, who was a kind and gentle man, said he thought it was probably just migraines; which was plausible given the amount of work I had at the time getting the King's Road building ready for the launch date, now less than a month away. He suggested I take some migraine medication and see how I got on.

But something in me felt it wasn't that. I had a feeling as he was suggesting that it was migraines that it was *not* that, that it was something else. What it was I had no idea, but I remember looking straight into his eyes and asking if I could please have some tests done, just to rule out anything else. He knew I wasn't a fusspot, as I hardly ever had needed to see him before, except for the odd, routine check-up. I have no idea why I felt so strongly about it, but that was how I felt at that moment. Clearly a little taken aback by my unexpected and rather forthright request, he studied me, evidently weighing something in my mind. Then he wrote out my referral for a series of blood tests.

My sister had insisted on coming with me to receive the results of my recent blood tests.

'Truly', I said to her, 'I really don't think it is necessary for you to come in with me'. It was a beautiful midsummer's day; there was a warm breeze in the air, and it was one of those days where the sky is wearing what looks like an enormous china-blue cap. It was the kind of perfect day that always makes me glad to be alive.

As I left my sister in the car park and headed into the hospital, all I could think about was how it was such a shame to have my appointment today, to be indoors and in a waiting room on such a beautiful day. It was 4 July 1996, and I was looking forward to getting back out into the afternoon sunshine and enjoying the rest of this lovely day with Karen on nearby Wimbledon Common.

I was directed to a consulting room. My eyes helped my mind quickly scope the space for the security of something familiar in an unfamiliar moment. I noticed the sunshine streaming in through the window and thought, *That's nice for people to come in here.*

My consultant looked up from studying my notes. After brief introductions, he gestured for me to sit. I took my seat so that my right shoulder was, to my delight, gently bathed in warm sunshine.

My doctor sat back in his chair, clutching his hands together in front of his solar plexus, and said, 'The good news is you look very well. The bad news is, I'm afraid you're not'.

My heart lurched. I had so many thoughts jostling and shoving at each other for position to come out and be heard first, but nothing came out. I sat there, staring at my consultant. I was on the fulcrum of a see-saw, my mind sparking with rapidly multiplying questions. Percentages? Risks? Hope? Good news – how good? Bad news – how bad? *I'm not brave enough to ask. Don't tell me this way. Slow down. Stop. Rewind. Which way now? What? How?* My thoughts trailed off as I tried hard to focus on his next words.

'Pardon?' I stuttered. I winced to avoid hearing any more of what he was telling me. I was being diagnosed with systemic lupus erythematosus (SLE), also known as lupus. Lupus, my consultant told me, is an incurable autoimmune illness in which the immune system mistakenly attacks healthy connective tissue and organs. It causes chronic inflammation, which affect the skin, joints, kidneys, heart, brain, and nervous system. Lupus is also known to gradually worsen over time, and the damage to major organs can be life-threatening.

I didn't get all that at the time, but I heard enough to know that the bottom of my world had just fallen out. I heard just six words: incurable; life-threatening; major organs; brain. The final word that I remembered him saying, about the brain being at risk, sent a jolt through me. If something attacks the brain, the master control, it doesn't bear thinking about the outcome.

My consultant calmly continued. 'Your blood tests show you have extremely high levels of antibodies'.

The ramifications of this diagnosis and what might happen if my antibodies attacked any of my major organs were made clear to me again: in short, life-threatening.

He continued. 'We have to monitor your blood tests very closely now'.

He then said something which I'd never heard of or, to be honest, had even contemplated before. "Seventy-five per cent of illnesses I see in my practice are stress-related. To give yourself the best chance to cope with your diagnosis, you need to learn to manage your stress …'

That's odd, I thought. *I didn't even realise I was particularly stressed.* I suppose I was stressed. I must have been. Certainly setting up any business was stressful, but I thought that was all par for the course, and I was relatively young, in my early thirties. Other than the recent sharp pains behind my right eye and blurred vision, I didn't feel like or realise that I was particularly stressed, either mentally or physically.

In fact, I was at last enjoying the point to which I had brought my business. I felt that the amount of focus – and, I guess, stress – over the last six years seemed somehow worth it, and normal. *It was just what you did,* I thought. *You keep pushing, striving. It's just what you did, wasn't it?*

As I mulled over my consultant's last sentence, one word anchored itself into my mind: stress. All at once it made sense. *That's it,* I thought. *That's what I need to do.* Doing a reasonable attempt at coaching myself into grabbing an opportunity, I continued: *Yup, that'll be fine, I just need to manage my stress.*

I was momentarily buoyed up by the fact that I had, so I thought, alighted on a solution. Shortly afterwards, another thought crashed in:

I hadn't the faintest idea about how to go about managing stress. Never mind. Clearly my doctor would have the solution, I reasoned. After all, he'd suggested it.

So I said, 'That sounds like a great idea. I can do that. I can manage my stress, I'm sure'. I paused before fumbling with my words. 'So *where* do I start?' I stammered, ' I mean, *how* do I start? Where do I learn to do that?'

He simply replied, 'I have no idea, but if ever you ever do find out, let me know!'

I had a mixture of feelings crowding and shoving around in my head. The bits about the diagnosis that I did retain scared the living daylights out of me. The bit I held on to was that I had to learn to manage my stress, quick smart. I was under no illusion this was serious and likely to get worse. I was lucky that my consultant gave me a clue at least as to what I could do to help myself. But with no prior knowledge about the topic of stress or how to deactivate myself from its grip, it was clear I was on my own to find an effective plan for myself. I wondered if I would ever be able to let him know.

Stress as a concept wasn't something that ever registered on my radar before that day and certainly not as something that I could actually do anything about. Now that I had received the severity of this diagnosis. I *was* stressed. Officially. And royally. I had a progressive and overwhelming feeling that I was out of my depth. Looking back, I now realise it was the suddenness of it all that was the biggest shock. I felt the rug had been pulled from beneath me, and for the first time in my life, I felt I had totally lost my balance. I felt I had no control or knowledge over what was happening to me. Within my veins and organs, a battle was evidently in full cry. I had no resources at hand to know how to calm the situation, to disentangle my thoughts and emotions, to find my way back into balance again. Whatever that was.

I had not been feeling well for some time; that was true, but I thought I was otherwise fit and healthy. I thought I was just tired. I had a lot going on, but overall, I was full of positivity, which is why, I suppose, that it never got labelled as stress or a problem in my head. I hadn't considered at all that I could be *becoming* seriously ill and that it had most probably been happening for a while, my body being driven out of its state of balance by all the times I'd had undoubtedly unremitting periods of stress. After all, I reasoned, as I sharply woke from my inadvertent waking slumber, the more I thought about the journey I had taken over the last six years, the more it slowly dawned on me that it *had* been stressful. It *had* been a roller coaster of uncertainty; of striving; of never switching off properly.

Although I had never before stopped to dwell on it, I realise now that a pervasive thought was never far away; the chips are down on this business. If my business didn't work, I'd lose my house. It was as stark as that. Looking back, I can see now with absolute clarity that this would have been stressful – if not fully consciously, at least certainly subconsciously. If I felt on some level that my home was on the line, that's stress. Not recognising I was stressed was the first basic element that I'd overlooked. Once I'd missed that piece of the jigsaw, I couldn't even begin to do anything about finding ways to undo the stress or disengage from it.

I was used to ending each day thinking about what I had to do to generate business (subtext – if you don't you'll lose your home), and as soon as I woke up, I was back on it, thinking of ways to generate business (subtext – or you'll lose your home). Sleep. Wake. Repeat subtext. I now realise the subtext was always there. Sleep. Wake. Repeat.

I was walking a tightrope but hadn't realised it until now. I dared not look down. I knew it at some level, and my body therefore knew this too. I had worked tirelessly and tried to get the business into a position where the bottom line was protected as I knew this would give me breathing space to enjoy what I had created. Here I was, six years on; I had reached my breathing space, but it was too late to enjoy it.

I hadn't noticed the signs before – or perhaps I had ignored them: a headache here, poor sleep there, back tension here, leg pain there, pain behind my eyes, a life-sapping fatigue. None of it – in my busy mind, at least – added up to much to be concerned about. I always chalked it up as a transitory thing. I realise now I relied on my body to simply somehow sort itself out. Whatever I did or whatever life threw at it, I just expected it to right itself like a spinning top. It may wobble but it keeps spinning. It doesn't fall down. If it ever did, I would just pick it up and set it spinning all over again. It simply never factored into my thoughts that this was unhealthy.

To make matters worse, I didn't eat particularly well. Often, I skipped breakfast, grabbing a sandwich on the go whenever there was a five-minute break. I always had a coffee on the go and drank fizzy drinks like they were water. At home, often late, I'd rustle up something quick from the fridge or, more than likely, grab a takeaway on the way home. Once, I ordered my favourite meal from my local Chinese take-away. I was completing a drawing at the time for the King's Road launch, and when I finished the drawing, thinking it had been about half an hour, I jumped into the car and headed to the take away. I was met with surprise when I entered the place as they were closing.

They said in surprise, 'We were worried about you. We wondered where you'd got to. You rang your order in three hours ago!"

I had simply been too busy and engrossed in what I was doing to listen to my body's hunger pangs. My body was used to being ignored.

Around the same time that I was diagnosed with SLE, my best friend Dinah was diagnosed with bowel cancer. I remember trying to raise her spirits up as best I could, and she did the same for me. We edged each other on to get on top of our illnesses and emerge out the other side illness-free. We were young and just wanted to get on with life.

Increasingly, I found I didn't recognise my body's reactions any longer. I caught the back of my hand on something when I was moving a table, and it caused a small, insignificant-looking cut, not much more than a graze, really. By the next morning, the back of my hand had doubled in size with poison. It was an externally visible sign of what antibodies in overdrive were capable of doing to something as insignificant as a small scrape to the back of my hand. I began to wonder what was going on inside me.

One night, I found it harder and harder to breathe – sharp pains, like knives stabbing at me, consumed every breath. I had developed pleurisy. This time it was the lining of my lungs which were under attack. Frightened at the out-of-control nature of what was happening, I felt as if I was tiptoeing with my health. What or where would my antibodies attack next? How long would I get before the next attack?

My body was becoming a foreign land. I didn't know the terrain or the language or even how to find shelter. I felt increasingly like I was being wrenched from my moorings. With every symptom that flared up, I was alarmed at the speed and ferocity of the reaction in my body. Not sure where it would attack next, I developed a heightened state of alert and with no strategies to calm myself – body or mind – I realised I was now playing Russian roulette with my life.

The diagnosis was delivered two weeks before the launch of my King's Road gallery. The concept of now having to slam on the brakes on my business plans and undo all the invites and associated planning somehow seemed even more stressful than letting it carry on and dealing with what needed to be dealt with afterwards. Instinctively, my consultant seemed to understand the tightrope I was now walking. I was lucky.

In those days, I had private health care, and maybe what followed was only possible because of that, but I bargained with my doctor saying I needed to stay out of hospital as I had to launch my gallery. To my amazement, he seemed to understand and agreed, saying he would manage my health and monitor my blood tests regularly to leave me to concentrate on my launch.

But, he insisted, 'If your blood tests show that it is becoming too dangerous for you to be left untreated, you will *have* to come into hospital. Do we have a deal?'

I was actually driving past my local hospital – St George's University Hospital – at the time. I thought it seemed such a paradox, to be driving past the hospital whilst at the same time having this conversation with him. I said *yes, absolutely, thank you!* The show went on, but in the back of my mind was a certainty that I didn't want to continue with my business. Something had changed in me. I knew something had to change.

My life and work were inextricably linked. It was clear now that I had to find a new way to live with more balance, and central to that, find a way to manage my stress or, perhaps more crucially, find a way to undo the damage that had been done by years of stress. All I knew is that I needed to find a balance. I recognised now I had no choice. I clearly couldn't keep going straight ahead as I had been. In effect, I was forced to stop and to realise I was at a crossroads.

The gift of my childhood vision returned to me many times in life, usually when I was least expecting it. When I was in business, I knew I had numerous chances to take advantage of another person financially, which seemed the norm in business, but I found I never could. The dog-eat-dog world seemed to have a flaw in it. The moment I remembered I had a choice and it was bound up in something much bigger than the drive I had to gather as much as I could to build my own small wall of security, I was awake to the fact that options existed. With that realisation an immediate brake was placed on the automatic thought process that was driving me solely to a destination based on my personal financial security over every other consideration. However, knowing what I knew from childhood still caused me more than its fair share of angst as I had to exist in the material world. It is quite a balancing act to forego immediate financial stability – if the gaining of it felt wrong – and instead place my trust in a process that I understood in another way would sustain me, but at some point, who knows when? Perhaps in the next life.

I would often have an inner dialogue that would wrangle with the facts and ramifications, but always within that inner turmoil I was able to sense a faint beat within me that would let its presence be known. At those times, something in me fixed my internal resolve with a single-minded focus, as if I was on a tightrope, and, instead of looking down, I was aware that I needed to focus solely on the destination of the wire to reach the other side of the tightrope.

This feeling always gave a calm message, but it was never words, just a distinct feeling: 'It will all be all right'. It seemed to connect me to a higher sense in which I understood that I should trust and have faith.

The traces of my childhood message continued to filter into my life in myriad ways, large and small, throughout my life. Sometimes I got a sense that acted as an affirmation when I spoke to someone who, like me, used signposts and synchronicities to guide him or her through life. I always delighted in speaking with the few people who, in whichever way they did it, used internal navigational tools to connect to their bigger-purpose picture.

CHAPTER 8

Supper in Rome

In the autumn of 1996 I was still reeling from my diagnosis when I was invited by my business partner, Richard, to visit a potential client in Italy. I arrived on a flight from London to Pisa in the middle of a rainstorm. Once my taxi left Pisa Airport, the rain-soaked landscape became increasingly rural. Our route took in undulating lanes, guarded by trees already changed to their autumnal cloaks, their branches laden with leaves like fingertips in balletic poise, pointed down, a natural waterslide to revive thirsty soil below.

We passed through ancient stone villages, ribbons of smoke curling from chimneys. As we drove further inland, the damp, misty air slowly cleared to reveal hills braided with vines and gentle sloping valleys dotted with stout olive trees.

We arrived at our destination, an ancient mill now a Relais & Châteaux boutique hotel. As soon as I got out of the car, I took a deep breath, my nostrils drawing in a sublime "after the rain" freshness. I thought, *This is heaven.*

I knew I was coming to Italy for a few meetings, one of which was with the hotel's owners, who were looking to purchase some of my artists' sculptures. I arrived in a beautiful building with an age-worn flagstone floor, its wide staircase and soaring wooden roof constructed from ancient wood beams.

As soon as I saw the space, I forgot I was ill and was instead delighted to be there to help them select items that would enhance this extraordinary space. I found Richard and his girlfriend, Sharon, just finishing lunch. I was brought into a tall windowed room with floor-to-ceiling original glass-paned doors which ran along the length of two sides of the room. What surprised me at the centre of the room itself was a pond, complete with floating lily pads!

As soon as I greeted them, Richard smiled broadly and said, 'Do you want to come to Rome for supper tonight?'

'Wow, yes sure, that sounds amazing', I replied instantly, before adding, 'how far away is Rome from here?' I was familiar with northern Italy from my days with Benetton and their base in Treviso just north of Venice, but I wasn't familiar with Umbria, where I now found myself in Italy. I was pretty sure Rome was a long way south.

Richard, meeting my perplexed look as I mentally calculated where we were in relation to Rome, jumped in and said, 'There's someone we've been invited to meet'.

We arrived in the heart of Rome around six p.m. It had recently stopped raining, and the streets were glistening. We drove in thick Roman traffic, filing slowly past the Coliseum, its ancient columns and arches silently imposing, the keeper of stories we will never know. We were taken to the centre of Rome and then walked to a bustling area near the Spanish Steps known as Via Margutta. As we walked to the restaurant, we turned the corner, and I was told the filmmaker Federico Fellini had lived in this little street when he was young. At the end of the road on the right was a brightly coloured restaurant where there was a drinks reception.

As Richard, Sharon, and I mingled, we were introduced to Mikhail Gorbachev. As I shook his hand, there was no sense of arrogance as one might expect from a former world leader. Instead, he exuded a gentle warmth and peacefulness. As we all sat for supper, I had the great fortune to be seated next to Elio D'Anna. Elio, I soon discovered, is the visionary founder of the European School of Economics. Elio and I remained in deep conversation for almost the entirety of the evening. We spoke deeply about life and its array of synchronicities.

He said to me, 'The world needs heads of corporations and countries who have the *right* intention'. His vision in founding the school is to enable its students to be "pragmatic dreamers", and to educate them to elevate their thinking "for the greater good" and with integrity, not to just think about the short-term commercial gain of corporate business. He was the first person I shared about the vision I'd had when I was 6 years old and how it had shaped my own business life. It felt the right time to share what I had been taught. We both commented on and understood that conversations like the one we were having happened very rarely. It was fantastically reassuring to me to find a like-minded soul like Elio. It somehow seemed all the more poignant that Mikhail Gorbachev was with us that night in Rome too.

CHAPTER 9

A Turning Point

One can have no smaller or greater mastery than mastery of oneself.
—Leonardo da Vinci

'Seventy-five per cent of illnesses are stress-related. You've got to learn to manage your own stress'. These words, used by my consultant, shot into my awareness like a red flare in the sky. They seemed to keep reverberating in my head, as if a small child was tugging at me gently yet insistently for my attention. I felt as if this was a road sign to which I needed to pay particular attention. I realised I was fortunate to have had a consultant who gave me a clue that there was something to help myself, that I had a direction I could go to help address one of the known triggers for my particular diagnosis.

At some time in their life, most people have experienced some form of physical injury or pain, and sometimes experienced a more serious illness. We know, for example, that physical pain is a physiological response, a warning generated by the body to alert us that something is not right. The body's aim in signalling pain – or indeed many other symptoms – is to get our attention out of our head, laden as it often is with a never-ending monologue of plans or self-sabotaging thoughts and fears, and to get the consciousness back into an awareness of the body. The body's signals of pain are often an opportunity to reconnect and to discern what is causing or exacerbating the symptom. It is not always a physical reason, given the amount of traffic flowing through our minds and disrupting any hope of harmony, the dis-ease can be mental, emotional, or physical. It is like standing by the side of a busy motorway or intersection in downtown New York City, with all the horns and sirens blaring; the constant noise is an assault. We tune it out, but that doesn't mean the cacophony stops, as part of our brain hears it, processes it, and never switches it off. It just means we have learnt – mentally, at least – to screen out the noise from our conscious minds. Our bodies, and in particular, a part of our brain known as the hippocampus, doesn't switch off. Instead, it is part of our survival armoury and stays vigilant and hyperalert to all the elements within our environment that could signal danger. We have evolved to always be alert and primed ready for fight or flight, so because our physiology doesn't differentiate between real or imagined threats that run unchecked through our minds, it can cause all manner of mental firecrackers and explosions which simply result from our tickertape of random, often catastrophic or self-sabotaging thoughts.

Instead of taking this valuable opportunity to *listen* to my body, or to take time to try to understand what the cause might have been and therefore take steps to rectify the situation, all too often I would reach for medication in the form of painkillers to silence the pain or sleep medication to cope with my increasing anxiety that stopped me from sleeping. I effectively muffled the one thing that could bring me back to the core of what was troubling me and instead snuffed out that opportunity to carry on with my daily life. I was walking blindly in an assumption that my body would *somehow* cope regardless of what the mental environment looked or sounded like. Any thought for the care of my mind and its symbiotic relationship within my body was not on my radar. Bizarrely, looking back to my 30-year-old self with the benefit of hindsight, I can see I simply forgot about the impact on my body of years of stress, and it is shocking to realise that I took it completely for granted.

My body had simply run out of options to keep the show on the road; as it failed, it at last jolted me awake. I was left flailing for solutions, but in reality, I was already far behind the curve. Before I knew any better, I was extremely angry with my body for, as I saw it in those early days, letting me down! On top of my woefully misplaced anger, I realised I was totally unprepared for what to do. In that humility, I realised I had no means to actually help myself cope with my condition, let alone plan a recovery. In my hands I had a roughhewn block of stone that needed to become my new foundation. My first task – to find a chisel. I didn't know if my body would still be listening by the time I caught up, but I had nowhere else to be, so I began to work.

One summer evening, as I was driving over the river on my way home from work, I received a call from Dinah. She told me the chemotherapy she'd been having for her cancer hadn't worked. She calmly announced that she was stopping her chemo. 'It makes me feel too ill. I just can't do it anymore'.

There was a moment of silence as she waited for me to digest the enormity of what she was telling me.

I couldn't find the appropriate words. What are the appropriate words, anyway? 'Oh gosh, I'm so sorry. No. Please don't give up. Come on, Dinah, please fight this. I'm sure you'll find a way. Have you asked the doctors for another solution? There has to be a way'.

She was giving up. Across the distance and into the silence she added, 'There is no point, Suzie.' I couldn't believe what she was saying.

I pulled the car over and implored her to try to keep going, to find a way, perhaps something will work. I pleaded with her not to give up.

But she calmly said, 'No. My mind's made up, I'm going to concentrate on what time I've left. I want to have treatments that make me feel good, that make me feel peaceful'.

She continued. 'I know you won't believe it, but I've found having regular massage really helps with my pain, and it's the only thing that puts me in a peaceful place, so that's what I need. That's what I'm focusing on from now, Suzie, I need to stay peaceful'.

Dinah passed away peacefully a few months later. In my ignorance and very possibly my own denial at how ill she was feeling I was angry with her for – as I saw it at the time – not fighting the disease, but as time went on I found I admired her courage more. I admired the grace and clarity she clearly had at that time, and as she approached her final days, she knew what she needed. I respect her for that and although I didn't recognise it at the time, she taught me something vital about what is important for the spirit in the face of a terrible illness.

'I'm playing Russian roulette with my life', I blurted to my mother in a tearful phone call shortly afterwards.

My mother was the first person to introduce me to the idea of energy medicine. I was open to it as I'd heard of its success with horses but was very vulnerable and aware I might simply be clutching at straws, wasting my time, or worse, getting my hopes up, only to have them dashed again. I was extremely fragile, and I knew I couldn't take much more turbulence.

An interesting thing happened during my first session. I noticed I had become deeply peaceful. It was a great surprise to feel this peaceful, and it brought a wonderful feeling of liberation from the enveloping fear I had had since my diagnosis. In an instant, all my worries and fears were distanced beyond what seemed to be a surrounding "bubble". I felt aware of all my worries, but they felt so far removed from me that they all of a sudden had no traction in me. Many years later, when I was taking a course at Harvard, I heard about a state of being that patients can access called *remembered wellness*. I realised right in the moment of this intensely peaceful feeling that I had forgotten what it felt like to be well! In that moment, it served to give me a tangible anchor to a state of peace that was sadly long forgotten. This peaceful state that I had just reconnected with now created the impetus that reminded me of my goal: peacefulness. I had at last keyed back into a state of bliss that I hadn't even realised that I had forgotten existed; I realised in that moment that I had lost that serene feeling of peace and oneness which I would regularly tap into as a young child when I was surrounded by nature.

As my first energy session progressed, it brought a feeling of relief, as if a heavy weight had been lifted. This was quickly followed by a distinctive feeling, which I could only describe as an inner euphoria, as if I was a child doing cartwheels on the sand on the first day of a summer holiday!

I certainly arrived at that first session as a sceptic, however, but I left feeling without a doubt that a profound shift had just taken place. I felt lighter in my spirit. I can't put words to it, but it was at once a new feeling and also a very warm, familiar, and comforting feeling of bliss and contentment. It felt like I could at last give a deep sigh and relax into a comfy chair at the end of a long, tiring day.

That night I had one of the deepest and most nourishing sleeps I could ever remember, and when I woke, I had a feeling that a palpable transformation had occurred. Within my body was a feeling of being perceptively lighter and free, and my brain felt clear, as if a cloying, grimy mist had lifted. I continued to have weekly sessions, and the positive feelings from the first session seemed to compound. I felt a deepening sense of peace and well-being.

A few weeks later, I was scheduled to have another blood test. When the results came, my consultant told me, almost incredulously, that my antibodies had dramatically reduced. I recall him saying, 'This reduction is quite unexpected. So much so, it's as if we've had the wrong bloods from you all along!'

I wondered if this sharp and unexpected reduction in antibodies was a sign, a *positive effect* of something else that was going on. I wondered if it was caused by the core of me now being profoundly peaceful and if this could generate a subsequent change in physiological output. I wanted there and then to let my consultant know that between now and the last time I had had a blood test, I'd had a series of bioenergy treatments, but then I thought better of it. It was still the 1990s, and medical understanding of the more subtler forms of healing were limited. I didn't say anything, besides maybe I reasoned with my sceptical hat firmly wedged over my ears this could just be a blip in my bloods and at my next blood test my antibodies would most probably have skyrocketed again. I decided not to say anything at that time, but if the trend continued and I remained symptom free, I'd say something. I felt one day the time would be right.

Another positive effect I noticed following the energy treatments to my great surprise was that I now craved natural food! One day, coming back from work, I had forgotten to stop for lunch, again. Starving hungry, I stopped at a convenience store. I absentmindedly planned to grab a pack of crisps and a chocolate bar; my quick fix. I planned my choices as I parked the car. *Yup, that should do it*, I obliged with myself.

My mind was elsewhere, darting backwards and then forwards, alternating between a rush of thoughts that were at once processing events of that day and what that would mean to the following morning's workload. Before I knew it, I was projecting forward to what I needed to do tomorrow, creating a priority checklist that gave me the mental illusion that I was in control and therefore ready for the next day.

Luckily, I wasn't at a familiar store, so I had to concentrate. As I rushed past the fresh fruits and vegetables my eyes suddenly stopped on a large bag of brightly coloured green and deep red baby salad leaves. Without thinking, I put my hand down to grab the biggest bag I could find. When I got to the crisp and chocolate section, I was amazed that they didn't hold any interest for me at all. My body and mind felt satisfied; they had what they wanted. I couldn't wait to pay and get back in the car. As soon as I did, I ripped open the bag and ate mouthfuls of lettuce! I was as astonished as a passing pedestrian. My body, despite myself, was reclaiming precisely what it needed; it was at last in the driving seat.

During this time, I was fortunate to be recommended to some clinically experienced and very professional complementary therapy practitioners. With their guidance, and in tandem with the therapies that they provided, I was taught specific relaxation techniques so I could help manage my own stress. I liked this aspect; I didn't want to maintain my health or well-being only by relying on another person. It therefore resonated with me very early on that whilst the therapies were essential in jump starting my well-being recalibration, it didn't seem right that I should expect that state to endure if I didn't actively engage in ensuring I remained in the process myself. It seemed the tandem effect was the only way that my health could be sustained.

Even though I'd had my first few energy treatments and was blown away by how they made me feel, my old habits all too quickly crept back in, rather like a weed growing back when a gardener goes on holiday. I had still some rather detrimental habits to keep weeding. It was clear it was going to take a bit of time to break my absentminded habits and remember to tune in to my thoughts, to retrain some parts of my automatic thinking, to challenge my thoughts if they were dragging me off course, and to remember to intervene and actively switch my dials back to the right frequency for my body. If I was to stay automatically tuned in to this frequency, I had some work ahead of me.

The way I saw it at the time was that, rather like in classical architecture, the state of well-being was represented by the triangular pediment that sits on top of tall pillars. The pediment can't balance perilously on just one pillar. For me, the therapy process had two pillars. In my journey, the skill of the practitioners were one essential pillar which enabled me at times of great stress or distress to be gently guided back to a state of calmness, of peace – in essence, to a state of remembered wellness.

But the pediment of well-being needs at least a second pillar, sometimes more, depending on individual circumstances. The second pillar that I needed at that time for my own healing journey, was a self-help pillar, so I could be skilled up mentally and physically to help myself. The third pillar would be orthodox medicine. Somewhere between the pillars and joining them all was my doctor, who gave me a direct clue: I had to play my part, and the way I could best do that was to manage my own stress levels. There was no other way around this. In my experience both as a designer and as a patient, there needs to be at least three pillars in place to strengthen the integrity of the overall mind-body structure of health.

I remember in those early days telling one of my practitioners how angry I felt at my body for what I perceived to be letting me down. I was guided to understand that my body hadn't let me down at all; on the contrary. The practitioner helped re-educate me to realise that my body was doing, and probably for a long time had been doing, all that it could to get itself back to balance.

'Homeostasis', he continued, seeing that I was genuinely interested, 'is the natural of state of harmony the body will always try to return to, given the right set of circumstances. But if the environment, either mentally, emotionally, or physically, is not conducive, it is very difficult for the body to ever return to a perfectly attuned balance'.

I felt that what he'd just explained to me – coupled with the experience of peacefulness that had been accessible to me during the energy medicine treatments – somewhere contained in both experiences, something essential was slowly coming into focus.

I'd had a busy period with work and decided to take the weekend off. I didn't regularly buy a newspaper, try as my father might to convince me. He was always an avid newspaper reader and encouraged me to understand more of the world through reading it, but I never wanted to engage in the mainly negative spiral of news stories, as I saw it.

However, unusually for me this particular Sunday, I didn't question it as I just felt I wanted to read a Sunday paper and felt drawn to read its supplements. In one, an article caught my eye: a feature on Michael O'Doherty, one of the founders of Plexus Bioenergy, an Irish-based organisation. The journalist described having received a treatment from Michael with fascinating results.

I felt drawn to what I was reading, and first thing on Monday morning I called their office. I was resolved that I would have to travel to southern Ireland, but to my delight, I was told that they were going to be commencing training in London in a few months' time. I signed up and could hardly wait for the course to start.

I was increasingly interested in one of the main elements of the bioenergy training, which consisted of mornings and evenings learning an ancient Chinese meditation practice known as chi kung (pronounced chee-gong), also known as qigong. It literally means *energy* (chi/qi) *moving* (kung/gong). It is an ancient system of holistic healing which is based on traditional Chinese medicine. Its philosophy is that energy (chi), either mentally or physically, needs to flow and not be stagnant in order to be healthy in mind and body. Through a series of slow, specific co-ordinated movements and postures, as well as focused breathing techniques and visualisations, a calm, meditative state of mind is created with the aim of transmuting negative emotional states which, in turn, it is believed affect the physical body.

As I learnt and practiced the techniques taught by Plexus's chi kung trainer, Liam Fretwell, I noticed I was increasingly becoming more peaceful. I also noticed a corresponding improvement too physiologically, which was demonstrated in my stable blood tests and, most importantly, a reduction in symptoms.

The other aspect of the Plexus training was based on energy medicine. This was similar to the first energy medicine treatment I had received the previous year. Its effect on me was just as profound and reaffirmed to me that this was an important modality for my inner well-being. In 1998 I qualified with Plexus and very soon had a string of eager clients.

CHAPTER 10

Learning to Walk

It was early summer of 1999. I had retrained and was increasingly fascinated by the concept of the mind-body connection. I meditated every day. I practised chi kung daily. I had two clinics, one in South Kensington on the first floor of a peaceful cobbled mews near the Victoria and Albert Museum. My second clinic was in leafy Wimbledon Village at a retreat centre. It was lovely there, so peaceful and surrounded by a pristine garden tended by nuns. My clients could drive in through the wrought iron gates and park right outside the front door.

This layout was particularly important for one of my clients, who was in her mid-sixties and had made an appointment to see me due to a severe hip and back problem. Her condition made it impossible for her to walk without the aid of walking sticks. Of the two clinic venues, the Wimbledon Village location was the easier one for her to reach as her husband was able to drive her directly there and help her get to the door.

As I scanned her energy field with my hands, I felt the energy around her lower back and right hip particularly heavy. This was to be expected. So, as I had been trained to do, I focused on this area, but I focused on it for a much more prolonged period of time than I would usually have done. Somehow it felt especially significant for her issues.

After a short while, and whilst I was focusing on this area, she suddenly exclaimed, 'That's odd. The top of my big toe is suddenly hurting, and my right ear has just blocked up!'

Feeling that this might be related, but I wasn't yet sure, I asked if either of these areas meant anything to her.

Without hesitation, she replied, 'Well, I don't think so, but it is odd because as I've not thought about it for years, but now I'm thinking about it, it is the same toe that I injured when I was a young child!'

I continued to scan her energy field and sensed that this could somehow be related to her current back problem. I gently enquired if she would feel comfortable sharing with me what happened to her toe when she was a child.

She happily shared with me. 'I was sitting on a garden wall at my home. I was only about 5 years old at the time, possibly even younger, when suddenly the wall collapsed. I was unscathed, thankfully, but a large stone must have landed on my big toe or hit it, I don't know, but all I knew was that that it was excruciatingly painful'.

I gently asked what happened next, and she said, 'I limped back inside in a lot of pain, to tell my parents. But when I got to my mother, she was in floods of tears, as she'd just learnt that her own mother had died. Of course, my parents were completely preoccupied with the tragic news that they were dealing with, and I think they simply didn't hear me'.

She reflected once more, adding, 'I remember thinking though, at the time, why aren't they listening to me?' She added, after another pause, 'I realise now I was actually feeling' – she searched for the right word – 'unsupported', before adding, 'I remember feeling quite angry with them at the time for not hearing me or helping me'.

She paused again for a moment and then went on. 'My toe got a lot worse overnight, but my parents were now thinking about the funeral. In the end, it took about three more days before they took me to hospital to have an X-ray, to find that it was badly broken'.

She said she had totally forgotten this event. 'Of course, I now realise that my lovely parents were just so consumed with the sadness that they were feeling. It wasn't intentional I know, but I guess to my young mind at the time, I didn't feel I was being heard or supported'.

At that moment she reported her ear had suddenly unblocked and the pain in her big toe, had now completely disappeared.

I continued working in her energy field, but in her expression of that experience, I felt her energy field shift and become lighter. This lighter feeling was particularly evident now around her right hip and lower back. The session finished and she left the clinic. About fifteen minutes later, the retreat centre's doorbell rang. It was my client again. She was laughing as she told me she had managed to walk out of the building, and walked about a hundred yards down the drive. When she reached the entrance gates of the retreat, she suddenly realised she had walked further than she had managed in years – but she had forgotten her walking stick, having left it in my clinic room!

I continued to see her daily for four days, as was the protocol, and then monthly until she felt that she didn't need the bioenergy. A few months later, she came to see me in my South Kensington clinic. Her husband came in with her at the start of the session.

I asked how their day had been, and he shook my hand warmly and said to me, 'Do you know we have just had a wonderful walk around Hyde Park? My wife could never have done that before'. He looked at me earnestly and said, 'Thank you for giving me my wife back'.

I cannot know, of course, whether it was the treatment that helped create this shift, but I find it a fascinating case, and to me it highlighted the very real possibility that thoughts and experiences are stored in the body. I was able to test this theory many times after this, but this was the first time there seemed to be some connection to a repressed memory – in this case, physical injury and a childhood memory somehow locked into the body. In focusing on the symptom that was stopping her at that time (her hip), it had helped to provide a clue of the source of the issue through her sudden pain in her right toe precisely where an injury memory occurred sixty years ago. The temporary blocking of the ear perhaps enabled her to focus more sharply on what it felt like to not be able to hear, triggering the full memory of the locked memory event. I shall never know for sure, but what I knew was that this was a phenomenon that I felt warranted respect and further awareness.

A few years before this, one of the first books I read from cover to cover when I was first diagnosed was Louise Hay's *You Can Heal Your Life*. Not only did I find her story resonated very strongly with me, what fascinated me was her idea that there is a code – a so-called filing system – where the file of thought, event, or emotion is deposited in a specific area in the body. It was a revolutionary concept for me and was as if an internally resident detective suddenly awoke from a long slumber, sleepily rubbed her eyes, dusted off her hat and coat, grabbed her notebook and magnifying glass, and got to work. This element of communication between mind and body seemed to hold a key that I was looking for.

If there is the possibility of some sort of a mental-physical filing system – I purposefully say "some sort", as it has to be acknowledged that the concept of an accurate filing system hasn't yet been validated scientifically. However, science recognises the link exists, so we can follow that train of thought: that our thoughts and emotions influence our body. If I'm carrying a heavy load physically, day in and day out, it follows that I feel the weight of that load in my shoulders. Following Louise Hay's idea, therefore, that if instead of physically carrying a heavy load I am instead carrying a heavy "thought load", Louise's book seemed to say that that repeated "carrying a burden" becomes imprinted and eventually felt in specific locations in the body.

Whether it is actually correct or scientifically provable isn't any longer the point. What happened in me when I read this was that I discerned a sense *in me* of its validity and worthiness to be tentatively explored. Each step towards this, taken in the spirit of exploration, it may be right, it may not be right, but I wasn't afraid to let myself carefully explore this new landscape and push open a few doors and peer under a few rocks. Like an internal archaeologist, there was a lot of digging and sifting to be done. Fragments of something that might be of interest were carefully kept to one side for further scrutiny. Little by little, the pieces came together; the object of my focus became clear.

I was loving my new life. I didn't feel stressed; my blood levels confirmed what I knew from my own body; and my antibodies were doing their best to behave. I simply wasn't interested in going back in to any form of business but I was in the real world. I had been increasingly thinking, *What am I going to do for myself, at this point in my life, that makes sense of where I now find myself – and more than that*, feels *right*?

I felt something which was profoundly essential to my being was coming into focus. Since being diagnosed with lupus, increasingly, I had the nagging feeling that I was out of balance. More than that, I felt I was running blindly through life, like a hamster on a wheel. This pervasive sense eased the more I practiced meditation. It became apparent to me and my friends and family that something in me was shifting; this way of life was sustaining me.

CHAPTER 11

A New Direction Presents Itself

Inow I had an increasing feeling that I should sell my gallery in the King's Road and that it was time to take the next step. After a major life-changing diagnosis, the landscape feels forever changed. The more I reconnected with myself through energy work and meditation, the more I felt the futility of losing my energy, as I had been used to. Not that I didn't love designing, creating, and representing other artists whose work inspired me, but within me the season had changed; entering summer doesn't make spring any less important.

I had been deliberating for a good few months, and weighing all the pros and cons. I finally made the decision on a summer morning, I had to sell. I made the decision as I woke, and as I drove to work, I thought of all the steps I would need to take to prepare the ground to sell.

Almost as soon as I got to work in the King's Road gallery, the phone rang. 'Can I come round for coffee?' the cheery voice at the end of the phone asked. It was a lovely Swedish designer who I had worked with a lot when I was at the Imperial Laundry, but as these things happen, we hadn't been in touch for a couple of years.

I said yes, of course. I thought of all the things I needed to get on with, most of all the planning that I'd need to sell the gallery. I found, to my surprise, that I was thinking, *Listen, look out for it; there's a sign to be found in this conversation.* I had learned to recognise the feeling that came with these types of thought.

As we shared coffee and news of what we were both doing these days, she mentioned in passing that she had woken that morning with a strong feeling to make contact with me.

She exclaimed, 'I don't know why, but it was really a strong feeling to call you'.

I looked at her, the sense within me becoming stronger that this was somehow significant. We continued to chat, and at one point in the conversation, she mentioned a lady she had worked with the previous year who was an international art agent. I got a sense of something coming into sharp focus in my mind. It was as if my hearing suddenly took on a more acute dimension. As she spoke more about the work she had done with this lady the previous year, I got another strong sense that I should be paying close attention.

Not knowing what to expect, but with a sense that I had to ask, I said, 'Gosh, I've just had a thought. I don't suppose this lady would be interested in this gallery?' I added, 'I've literally just decided this morning to sell it!'

She made a quick call, and later that afternoon the lady popped by as I was leaving for the day. She was keen to have a quick look around and at the building. The moment she saw it, she loved it! The legal side of the sale was effortlessly completed a month later.

I started feeling progressively well. In addition to having qualified in bioenergy, I trained in some more of the therapies that I had received when I was first diagnosed. I first decided to train in neurolinguistic programming (NLP) as I was fascinated in the link between mind and body and how the two seemed to communicate. I was interested first to learn practical tools to shape my inner dialogue to be a more conducive influence on my body.

My first step was to sign up to train in a course in neurolinguistic programming. Then, a year later whilst on holiday, I received a reflexology treatment. I was in a beautiful spa overlooking the Andaman Sea in Indonesia. Actually, I'd wanted to try the other treatments on offer, but they were fully booked, so I agreed, a bit reluctantly, to have reflexology. I wasn't sure about it, mainly because my feet are ticklish and very sensitive, and I thought it wouldn't be possible to actually enjoy the treatment. How wrong was I!

In an instant I was brought into my body. I simultaneously felt a progressive relaxation wash over me. I felt my body reclaim a state of relaxation, and through that, it served to remind my mind how wonderful it is to be so deeply relaxed. It seemed there was a two-way dance between mind and body. With meditation, I focused on the mind to enable it to help my body, but here it was the other way around. What was more, it was just as effective at reaching my goal; to reconnect and achieve a deep state of relaxation so that my mind, but particularly my body, could plot its way through the detritus left by years of pervasive stress.

As soon as I came back to England, I researched training schools and what was involved in the syllabus. I was thrilled to find a reflexology school that was taught in a hospital about ten miles away. I pored over the school's website and was interested to note that a cancer nurse, Lucy Bell, had trained with this particular school and she, along with the support of her professor of oncology at Charing Cross Hospital in London where she worked, had presented the work to the House of Lords. I found the transcript of her presentation and read – and re-read – her speech, which articulated from a nursing, clinical, and human perspective the reasons why integrated medicine was important to support the whole patient.

This was enough for me to know; this was the school I wanted to train with. I rang the school and its principal, Maureen Burgess, answered the phone. I explained why I was interested in learning reflexology, and to my surprise she suggested I pop by to meet her that Saturday morning and meet some of the current students who were close to graduating.

I cleared my schedule and was there at nine o'clock sharp. Maureen kindly let me sit in on the morning session. Students sat in a semicircle, and I took up my place next to a lady who was called Jo. The tutor was taking them through revision for their anatomy and physiology exam, which was to be in a few weeks' time. I was struck by the students' engagement and level of understanding of the complex physiological systems of the body. I realised I had a lot to learn.

CHAPTER 12

Coming to Hospital: an Unexpected Route

Exactly one year had passed since selling my business. I had sold it with sufficient funds to be able to take a sabbatical from work for the year. I was clear I didn't want to use my time going back into any sort of business. Instead, I used my first year to volunteer and gain further experience with my practice. However, I always knew when the year was up I would need to be pragmatic and top up funds to pay for things over Christmas. I also reasoned it would give me time to think what my next step would be for the coming year.

I had a plan. I would go to a temporary agency in my local town of Wimbledon and offer my curriculum vitae, but on the proviso that I was first and foremost interested in my clinics. So whilst they should look at my CV, they should also ignore it; I was clear there was nothing in my CV that I wanted to draw me back into business.

Looking more than a little perplexed, the lady from the agency agreed to my unusual set of criteria. She said, 'Are you sure you want us to take you at your word?'

To which I replied, 'Absolutely!'

Looking a little worried, she said, 'We have a temporary administrative position on one of the cancer units of St George's Hospital'.

I don't know what I was expecting, but I wasn't expecting to be offered any sort of job in a hospital. After all, I had tried only a few years earlier to stay out of this hospital when I was a patient. An odd thing happened, because I don't recall saying yes (left to my own devices, I probably would have said no and asked for them to try to find me another area in which to work).

Instead, it was as if I momentarily found myself in a bubble where I couldn't hear anything and couldn't remember what I had said, but clearly I did say something, as the next thing I heard was, 'That's great! Do you want to start tomorrow?'

At first I thought, *Whoa, I haven't said yes!* Realising I must have, I felt I needed a little more time to process what I had clearly just agreed to. So instead of starting the next day, it was agreed I'd start the following Monday.

I went home and suddenly felt more than a little confused that somehow my own life and the choices I had made had brought me to this point. Suddenly I couldn't see what any of it was for or what, if anything, my whole journey through illness and recovery was actually meant to be about. All of a sudden my confidence in my ability to discern my way through life suddenly evaporated. I felt shattered. I felt confused. I felt stupid for following so blindly this "faith" that I had in my ability to navigate life while holding to the memory of a vision and a teaching I'd had nearly thirty years before. I suddenly felt overwhelmed.

A friend came to visit me and tried to understand what I was doing with my life. He urged me to be careful. He was fearful, I think, that I was losing my mind because my choice to sell my gallery and to give up all that I had built seemed bizarre at the time. Who in her right mind, after all, spends all her energy to build something and then walks away from it?

I decided out of the blue to phone my lovely former boss at Benetton. I tried not to burst into tears but blurted out to him, 'Piero, I think I've messed up my entire life'.

I will never forget his response: 'Suzie, you need to remember that success is not in never falling. Success is when you pick yourself up after each time you fall'. His kindness and calm and accepting words found a resting place in me despite my increasing panic.

In that moment, I was able to regain my balance a little, as if the tightrope I was on suddenly stopped swaying, and I could find the focus to regroup and then plan to take the next step.

It was a bright, cold, sunny December day. I walked into the hospital still confused as to how my life and choices had just delivered me here. This, I kept reasoning with myself, is temporary – it was only for three months. I was met by the lady from the temporary agency at the hospital, and we walked together to the Ruth Myles Unit, which, I discovered, was the hospital's specialist haematology and bone marrow transplant unit. My inner tug of war was fully manned, tugging me this way, tugging me back that way.

As I walked into the hospital that day, wondering on one level what on earth I was really doing there, immediately countered with a thought that something would be revealed to me. At that moment, I had a feeling of deep calm, which carried with it a sense that I was to focus on the destination at the end of the tightrope rather than constantly look down. All I had to do was quieten my mind and deeply concentrate on each step that I was to take towards the end of the tightrope. It seemed clear to me that something crucial was going on, and somehow I just needed to be *present* and *focused* and then to *sense* the guidance that seemed to be nudging me. Coupled with this new sense of awareness, a recurring thought had folded itself into my brain: *three months will be a sufficient time.*

Over lunch on my first day, I was lucky to be sitting in the staff room at the same time as one of the senior nurses. She was taking a brief lunch break after an extremely busy morning. We chatted generally, and she asked me about my former work. She was very interested to know more about the therapies that I was now trained in.

She said, 'We need something like this on this ward. Our patients are here for such a long time, and the chemotherapy makes them feel so ill. It's very tough for them, you know, to keep positive'.

We agreed that it would be wonderful to offer some therapy

support to their patients, but in the same breath, we both knew this would be almost impossible. It was December 2000, and the general medical and scientific perceptions in the country and of many in senior positions within the NHS regarding the use of any type of integrated or complementary therapy, we both knew, were fairly hostile. We both knew also that trying to set something up like this would be almost impossible because of the red tape involved.

However, I was cheered up by the conversation, and as I walked home that evening, I could think of nothing else. I thought, *Here I am in one of the leading university school hospitals in the UK, and I now find I'm on a ward where patients are clearly extremely unwell.* The orthodox treatments they were being given – though life-saving – were extremely tough for patients to cope with during their treatment and isolation. This had just been voiced by an experienced and clearly compassionate nurse.

I was heartened to learn through my first chat with a senior nurse that she understood the potential benefits of therapeutic support for the quality of life of her patients. *But,* I countered with myself, *this is too unorthodox, and it's the NHS.*

From everything I'd read or heard about in the press, with a few exceptions, it was apparent that the medical profession at the time was not ready for this type of support being introduced. I was under no illusions. But I could see that if a project was designed, developed, and evidenced in the right way, this could be of help and support to very sick patients. It was also apparent that this nurse wasn't threatened by the concept of adding therapies to the care of her patients; on the contrary, she seemed to believe it would not only be more humane for her patients but could fill a void in her work as a nurse, as it would mean that her patients would get the human element of care that very busy nurses couldn't often find the time to do.

I got the feeling from her and many other nurses with whom I spoke after this initial conversation that what they were missing in their busy roles was what they referred to as an *essential element of care.* So many nurses told me it was this element of care which was the reason they came into nursing in the first place. I pondered: *A therapy project could be designed in the right, most professional way; it could be run fully under the guidance of nurses so that it would run in tandem with orthodox care.* This was not only possible, the holistic benefits seemed clear.

On the other hand, I couldn't ignore the vociferous opinions coming from some areas in the medical community and in the press at the time. This, I understood, would be no easy task, and this new environment was quite unlike anything I had ever experienced before.

That evening, I meditated on the conundrum. During this particular meditation, I received a strong sense that I should ask for help. I was reminded, in a flashback, to what I had been shown to do all those years ago as a child. I had a strong feeling as a result of that meditation that the act of asking for help would help me discern the next step. That was all I knew. What became clear during that moment provided me with what I would describe as a clarifying message. It was the feeling that I would somehow receive an intuitive sense or *recognition* of the first patient that I was there to help. I had a strong feeling that I would recognise that patient and that he or she would be the key to opening up some of the barriers that lay ahead.

In addition to understanding this element of recognition, the guidance within the meditation made itself clear. In order to be doubly sure of who this first patient was, I would be asked one clear question by someone related to that patient. This part was a "code", but it was clear it was the second part of the steps of recognition of the right first patient. The precise question I was looking out for was that that person would ask me, 'What do you do?' That was the exact sentence.

I mulled over all that I had just received. Since childhood, I was familiar with the clarity and the distinct feeling that higher guidance brings. In other words, I knew I hadn't made this up. I recognised instantly the *stilling* feeling that accompanied the message. I was surprised by the absolute clarity of the two steps and the precision of the key sentence that would, as I understood it, guide me to the first patient. It was, at the same time, humbling and a bit worrying; I was being asked – as I understood it – to trust everything on these two steps, and to ask of the nurses something which, up to then, was deemed somewhat if not totally impossible at the time.

There was a lot at stake, and if I looked at it logically, it was an enormous mountain to climb. There was a big part of me that was worried, especially as I really did not understand the landscape that I was now being guided – it seemed – into. I could believe that I might get a sense of a patient that I might be able to help through bioenergy. I had busy clinics, and I had seen how it had helped transform many patients. But to imagine that someone related to a patient would somehow pick up the same "coded message" and ask me the precise words, 'What do you do?'

On another, rational level, it seemed totally unlikely that these two circumstances would present themselves in relation to one patient. I had no logical reason to believe any of this could happen. Each time I pondered myself into self-ridicule for taking this notion of "guidance" seriously, my thoughts immediately overlaid with a veil of stillness. I was brought back again and again to a calm, accepting focus. The constant message remained unchanged: *This is what will be.*

I understood the complex snakes- and ladders-type landscape in which I was now working. This landscape consisted of minute steps forward, whilst multilevel clearances and management agreements, medical agreements, and business plans were written and signed off, or not, by numerous stakeholders. Then there were risk assessments and the thorny old and to some degree valid issue of 'where's the evidence?' Evidence comes mainly because large corporations invest and then reap the rewards of research. Not many organisations – at that time especially – were interested in an equivalent, funded research focus on innovative disciplines under the wide umbrella of integrated health. I knew if I landed on that particular topic, my efforts could – depending on beliefs and perceptions of who you were talking to – be back on the snakes and ladders board, moving forward or back with a thump, to square one.

When I looked, a pretty insurmountable mountain to climb lay ahead of me. I questioned again, and this time my extraneous thoughts jostled for position. In business mode, I weighed the pros and cons and the risks and benefits and not least the energy to drive this thing in any direction. The journey I had been on to this position – I had to admit – was unusual. I asked again, was I meant to be *here* in *this* hospital, at *this* time, and with *this* task? The same clear and yet certain message permeated effortlessly into my mind, instantly bringing with it an unmistakeable calmness and focus.

CHAPTER 13

What Do You Do?

A few weeks later, the ward was being prepared for Christmas. Tinsel was draped around the notice boards, and foil stars dangled in jaunty shapes in hallways. Christmas cards started to appear and were homed on swathes of ribbon along the corridor. I heard there was to be an emergency admission of a 28-year-old man, who was due in that evening by ambulance from another county outside London. I had heard he had acute leukaemia, which had relapsed after only six months of being in remission. His cancer was aggressive, and he was being admitted to our unit. If his condition did not stabilise, he would be transferred to the hospital's intensive care unit.

I was leaving the ward for the evening, and just as I got to the double doors at the exit, two ambulance crew brought in a young man on a stretcher. I looked at him, but he didn't make eye contact with me. My heart went out to him. It was all I could do right then.

The next morning and, as part of my role on the ward, I went to speak to every patient on the ward. When I got to this young man's room, I needed to ask him a few questions. As we spoke, I got an extremely strong sense that this was the patient I was to look out for. I said nothing but just noted my feeling.

He was clearly in distress. He was, understandably, a mixture of anger, fear, and frustration; he was sad and terrified. He told me he felt he had lost faith in his body. He explained he had only been in remission for six months: 'And now this, it's back again. I don't even know how I can bear more chemotherapy. It nearly broke me before, and …' His words trailed off.

He looked out the window for a moment. He looked back at me. 'I mean, this has come back so quickly'. His eyes were full of sadness. He looked down, frustrated, at his formerly fit body, which now as he saw it, was failing him again.

I looked at the bag above him. Every second it delivered intravenous chemotherapy directly into his body. It was his only hope right then, but he had lost faith in it to bring a positive outcome. He stared out the window again, clearly in thought, his face crumpling under the weight of his thoughts.

He returned to look at me, his eyes conveying the desperation and hopelessness of his thoughts. He softly added, 'It didn't work last time, did it?'

The type of leukaemia he had was known to be extremely aggressive, more so in someone as young as he was. It was heart-breaking to hear the enormous challenge that this young man was facing now, so soon after having endured it all for the best part of the previous year and having been in remission for only a few short months.

Inside his isolation room where he now lay, the metronomic beep-beep of monitors was his only companion. Outside, we heard the cheery sounds of the ward staff and visitors who were busy chatting, putting up Christmas decorations, and sharing laughter and stories. As their joviality wafted through the door separating him and them, it somehow only served to compound the tragedy unfolding just a few feet away. He knew that, at age 28, if he made it through this Christmas, it would almost certainly be his last.

Even though I had a persistent feeling that he was the patient I was to be helping, I hadn't received the second part of the code; I was suddenly professionally torn by the situation. I felt certain there was some support I could offer him, at least to try to calm his breathing. I wasn't thinking of anything more, but I thought, *He needs to stay calm.*

The next day his condition had worsened, and he was edging closer to renal failure. In addition, the righthand side of his face was swollen, and he was having difficulty speaking as a tooth had become infected due to his failing immune system. With leukaemia, cancer cells generated in the bone marrow are pumped out throughout the body, essentially firing blanks at any infection as the white blood cells, which would normally be produced in the bone marrow to do the job of fighting infection, become overwhelmed by the proliferation of cancerous cells within the blood. In conditions like this, any infection, including the common cold, can be fatal as the body has no immunity from any infection, putting ever more pressure on the body's vital organs. His doctors and nurses worked through the day and night to try to stabilise his condition.

As I spoke with him, I heard his resolve fading. I spoke with the senior nurse I had spoken to on my first day. I asked what I should do to try to get the clearance in place to treat him. She admitted she didn't know but suggested I speak with the ward sister. I explained to the ward sister what I was trained in, about my clinics, that my insurances and professional memberships were in place. I tried to convey that I was serious and not a flake, or, as I call them, carrot-in-the-hair type of practitioner who would make false promises or create false hope. I explained that my only plan was to help calm his breathing and therefore, through that, help calm his distressed body.

She listened attentively but then wasn't sure what to do. She asked for more information, which I immediately provided. She asked the young patient if he wanted some support through the type of therapy I was offering. He immediately said yes. She explained that she wasn't sure if she could get this in place, but she reassured him that she'd try.

A few days passed, and she said she still needed time to think about my proposition. She was clearly wrestling with it, trying to work out what to do for the best for her patient, yet hardly knowing me and being in a medical, evidence based environment. I absolutely understood and appreciated her very real dilemma. Both she and I did our best to explain to this young patient how difficult it was for her to make the decision, but I reassured him as best I could that she was trying hard to find a way. There was nothing I could do but wait and hope.

Four days before Christmas, his condition worsened, and it was clear that soon he would be transferred to intensive care. I was in the ward's kitchen making myself a cup of tea when at the open door the young man's mother appeared.

I thought she was about to ask me for a cup or some sugar as she said, 'Suzie, can I ask you a question?'

I finished stirring my tea and looked up at her. 'Of course. How can I help?'

She looked straight at me and without hesitating said, 'What do you do?'

Years later, she and I were talking about this, and she told me, 'I don't know why I said to you that day, "What do you do?" I felt so silly. I meant to say something completely different to you, but for some reason that's what I said!'

As soon as she said it, I recognised it was the code I'd been looking for. I didn't hesitate. I went straight to the back room where I found the ward sister drawing up chemotherapy for another patient.

I looked straight at her, and with an energy that seemed to come through me, I said, 'Unless you have a reason that I can't treat this patient, I need to start to see him now'.

She looked at me, a little shocked at my directness. She paused for a moment, as if weighing up the numerous pros and cons associated with her decision. She looked at me, and I looked straight back at her for what seemed a while but probably was only a matter of seconds.

She said, 'OK, Suzie, that's OK. Please go ahead'.

I started the first of his three treatments there and then, the third of which finished on Christmas eve. I went home to the country for Christmas with my family, but we'd agreed that at a specific time on Christmas Day I'd send him a remote session. There would normally be a break then in treatments, and it was agreed I'd see him when I returned from the new year break. I had to trust in my training, and trust in the process.

I came back to the ward early after the New Year's Day holiday, and I immediately looked into his room. My heart sank. Another patient was in his room. I scrabbled around trying to find his notes. They were gone. Had he gone to intensive care? Was he still alive? I stopped my thoughts mid-flow. There were no nurses at the reception; they were already busy with their patients. I waited for what seemed an eternity.

At last the ward sister came to the reception and said, 'Did you hear?'

I remember studying her expression. It wasn't downcast. Could she have not realised that I was wanting to know what had happened to this young man? I was surprised by her tone. I thought it was definitely more upbeat than I was expecting if the next sentence was bad news. I was sure she was talking about something else, so I said, 'No, what? I haven't heard anything'.

She looked at me, smiling, and said, 'It's your patient. He suddenly improved. He went home on Boxing Day'. She added, 'We need to talk in my office in ten minutes'.

When we met, she said to me, 'I don't know if you know what happened to his bloods, but he was due to go to ICU when suddenly, he improved. I don't totally understand what you do, or how you do it, but all I now know is we need this here for our patients, Suzie, on this ward'.

She continued. 'Can you please put this together as a project? I want to propose it to our business managers. I'm not sure about the doctors yet – we might need you to fly under the radar for a while – but leave them to me for now. All I know is our patients need this'.

Later that day, I received a pack of blood tests forms which in my day job role I had to file. Amongst the pages of blood tests were the test results for this young man. On the top righthand corner was a handwritten note by the haematology scientist who was responsible for checking blood results, which read, 'Technically in remission'.

CHAPTER 14

Healing Sounds: Part 1

I continued with the meditation and relaxation techniques I had been taught by Liam during my time studying Plexus bioenergy. I increasingly felt a great affinity with chi kung, not only as a means to help me continue to develop and deepen my inner practice and self-awareness but crucially as a means to help me stay as symptom free as possible from my autoimmune condition.

Sometime after I trained with Plexus, I was lucky to find a chi kung master in London. Ironically it was in South Kensington where, many years before, I walked past this particular door every day on my way to and from the underground station when I had my first gallery at Number 90 Fulham Road. The chi kung master I found, Sifu Simon Lau, was born in China and transmitted his classes with directness and deep wisdom. Our class would last between one to two hours, where we would learn specific "opening" arm movements, which were said to open up the energetic pathways. Following that, we stood for an hour or sometimes more, holding one specific pose with a singular focused attention directed to the dan tien, an area behind the navel which it is believed, with practice, energises the whole energetic system.

In tandem with the powerful chi kung techniques I was now

learning with Sifu Lau, one of the many aspects of chi kung that first drew me towards it was that it is centred on a regard for nature which is seen as a positive role model for life. Perhaps it resonates with me because of my childhood love of nature. Perhaps it resonates for another, deeper reason. I don't know.

I felt particularly drawn to practice a technique known as the healing sounds that Liam had shown us during our Plexus training. What I found so marvellous about this ancient practice was learning the five element theory. In this practice, the student learns how to focus on each major organ; how it is affected by both negative and positive emotions; and how to use imagery of the seasons, colours, and sounds to strengthen mind and body. Each major organ, it is also said within this ancient Chinese system, has an affinity not only with a specific season and colour but also an element, even a mineral and planet. It is also believed that for health to be sustained, each organ in the body needs to coexist in balance with all other organs in the system. Taking the same reasoning, if one organ or emotion is out of balance, it has a disharmonising influence on organs and emotions that depend on it in the cycle. Thus, to help counteract disharmony, in chi kung's healing sounds one can focus on the major organ that is known to be out of balance or on a negative emotion as a way to clear the energetic impact of that emotion on the mind-body connection and help bring about a sense of harmony.

Around this time I was referred to see a patient for help with advanced, incurable lymphatic cancer. He was understandably very sad about his prognosis and what the next stages of his disease would bring. I saw him weekly for bioenergy and talked him through the healing sounds. He was particularly drawn to doing them and in particular to focus on the healing sound for his spleen. In his guided sessions, I would ask him to think of the Indian summer, which, in Chinese theory, is said to be associated with the spleen, guiding him to use all his senses to bring to mind the rich, golden colour associated with the late summer sun and of fields of ripened corn at harvesttime. He really embraced the healing sounds and became proficient in it, practicing as often as he could. He said it made him feel extremely peaceful.

I had to travel to Australia as one of my friends was unwell, but when I left him on the cancer ward, I said to him, 'I'll see you when I'm back'.

As soon as I returned, I tracked where he was and found that he had recently been transferred to intensive care. I wanted to keep my last words to him, that I'd see him when I was back. I was sure that if he was unconscious he'd not know if I visited or not, but something in me felt it was important to honour my word.

I went to the intensive care unit, where I was already known to the nurses (from having seen other haematology patients who had been transferred there previously), and after introducing myself to the nurse looking after him, I asked if I could sit beside him.

He was unconscious and on an artificial respirator. I wasn't quite sure what to do or say. I took a moment to still myself and then quietly in my mind tried to connect with him, simply to say it was an honour to have met him and to have worked with him. I wanted to wish him well on his journey. I said I believed he soon would understand a whole lot more about the world than any of us on this plane could possibly know, and I finished by saying my only wish was to know he was OK. I finished by saying simply and humbly from my heart to him, *Goodbye. It was an honour to have worked with you.* After that, I left intensive care and went back to the haematology unit to finish my day.

I was sad, absolutely. I just hoped that what I had been able to impart to this brave man was enough. That evening I went for a long walk on Wimbledon Common, which was not far from where I lived; I just needed to be in nature. That night I had a dream, and it was of this man. He was lying on a hospital bed, with a doctor working hard trying to save him.

Suddenly he sat up and then he got up, though the doctor remained there with his body on the table. I then became aware that I was standing next to him on his right as he stood on what seemed like a stage. From here I could see in front of the stage a group of about twenty people who were all sitting patiently on chairs in neat rows arranged in a semi-circle. About four rows back, a lady suddenly seemed to recognise him. She jumped up, and with the same joy and ecstasy as one would a loved one you have been separated from for a long time, she ran towards him and they embraced. She was so full of love for him and seemed to me she had been waiting for him. The joy on her face and in everything about her was pure happiness.

The next thing I realised I was walking on his left. I looked down, and to my amazement we were walking through a field of corn. From where this dream started – where he was being worked on by the doctor, to the stage and his reunion, to then walking through the field of corn, I realised he had taken me on a circle. As we walked through the field of corn, we were returning to where his body still lay on a medical bed, with the doctor seemingly oblivious to the fact that he was not there.

He looked at me, smiling, and said, 'You see? They don't know everything, do they?'

I woke up with a start. As soon as I got to work, I checked with the intensive care team. He had passed away early that morning. To this day that entire dream is as vivid to me as it was then. I shall never forget it, but I can't know if it was just my own subconscious mind somehow processing the visit to him in intensive care, knowing about the therapy and visualisation work that he and I had done together and in particular his love of the Indian summer visualisation and the fields of corn. Maybe it was just my mind's way of processing and finding resolution in a final wordless goodbye in a harshly lit clinical room, with only the pointed beep of his heart monitor and rhythmic hiss and click of the artificial respirator. From my vantage point, I can't know.

After my first young patient went home unexpectedly, two young nurses came to ask me about what I did and the therapy I was trained in. They were keen to understand more. Catherine, a lovely, gentle young Canadian nurse, was particularly drawn to the energy medicine side of what I practised. I gave her a few treatments, and we talked a lot about it. She tried to find a course where she could learn to train in bioenergy, but frustratingly for her at the time they were now only running in Ireland. So, as this was too difficult for her to organise with her hospital rotas, she made enquiries about learning Reiki instead. She completed her level 1 and 2 and used to tell me excitedly how much she was enjoying having this wonderful therapy for her own sense of well-being but also for her friends and family.

Around the same time, during my lunch breaks or in any quiet moment we had on the ward, I enjoyed chatting with Louise, a dynamic, no-nonsense sort of nurse. She always brought her A game to the ward and her work. She had a sixth sense about her patients; in everything she did she just was efficient. She asked me to give her a bioenergy session, which I gladly did. In that session she said she felt drawn to the relaxation techniques in particular.

A few nights later, she was on night shift and one of her patients with terminal leukaemia was suffering with excruciating pains through the night. In the morning, when I came to the ward to work, Louise was still there having finished the handover and was about to go home to sleep. However, before she left, she said she wanted to share with me what had happened the previous night.

Around midnight her patient was in huge amounts of pain, and she had already given him the maximum dose of pain medication possible. Nothing was working. She had called the on-call doctor and despite his efforts, nothing could stop her patient writhing with the most terrible abdominal pain. In the middle of this, she suddenly remembered the breathing technique that I had talked her through in her own session a few days earlier. I hadn't even taught it to her with a view to her offering it to anyone else, it was simply an element which was part of her session. As she had had such an interest in it, she said that she'd remembered it well.

When no pain medication could break through her patient's excruciating cancer pain, she suddenly remembered the breathing technique. She gently started to talk him through the steps and to her – and his – great surprise, he noticed his pain reducing. He went from screaming the place down to softly breathing and then falling asleep.

She was so excited by this revelation that she couldn't wait to share it with me in the morning. She said, 'Go talk with him; he'll tell you all about it'.

He was an amazing guy. He'd had a very tough life and had spent time sleeping rough on the streets. He had a penchant for swearing, so I'll warn you now, although what follows is the sanitized version.

I gently knocked on his door and waited for his shout. 'Come in!' he bellowed. He had a big grin on his face, and I asked him how he was.

He said, 'Never better. That stuff you taught Louise – blimey – it effing well works!' He held out his hand to shake hands. I was honoured to do so.

He looked at me intensely and added, 'Thank you, I can't tell you how amazing it feels to have some control over this blxxxy cancer. Yeah', he said, nodding with his whole upper body and head. 'It feels absolutely brilliant, thank you'.

I demurred from the outflowing of gratitude as I felt it was really Louise who deserved it, and he said, 'Yeah, she's blxxxy awesome too. Couldn't have got through last night without her'.

What always humbled me was how the nurses on the ward embraced what I was doing. There was never the feeling from the nurses that this was something in conflict with what they were tasked to do. They were always so busy, so pressured but always had time to discuss a case with me, or give me the head's up on a patient they'd like to refer to me.

It was a little different, in those early days, with a couple of the young doctors who would be on rotation, and for some, our ward was just one of their stepping stones in their upward career trajectory. I remember one junior doctor going to see one of my patients early one morning.

The next thing I remember, the young doctor came barrelling out through the doors of the bone marrow transplant unit. As she passed me, she spluttered, 'I wish people would stop messing about with my patients'.

Sensing a little too much hostility and that it was most likely directed at me, especially as I was the only one at the nurses station as she thundered past, I decided to take myself off the ward for a short while, to let the dust settle a bit. I went to see that patient later in the day, and he said she had come in to see him just as he was doing his meditation. He was another strong-minded patient. He didn't have time to waste. When he woke up, it was his decision to start the day with a meditation. So, not wanting to be disturbed, he had simply asked her to come back a bit later.

That doctor made a point of finding me on her last day before she rotated off to another hospital, and to her credit, she said, 'I can see now what help you're offering to patients. It's really important. I can see that now'.

I was lucky in those early days as we had two wonderful, world-renowned consultants, the department's professor Ted Gordon Smith, and Dr Bevan, a consultant for sickle cell disorder. Neither consultant seemed to be challenged by what I was offering. They both actively supported me.

Dr Bevan was a renowned consultant in sickle cell disorder, a life-threatening genetic condition affecting people, mainly with African heritage. Dr Bevan was held in almost hero status by his patients for everything he did for them, which was wonderful to observe.

One day he came up to me and said, 'I'd like to speak with you. Have you got time in half an hour?' To my surprise he told me about how he'd heard about my work with one of the leukaemia patients from a nurse, and he said they were impressed as this patient had been able to have a procedure without insisting on extra medication simply by using the breathing techniques I'd taught her. This was something they'd never managed to achieve with her before, he told me.

He went on to say he had one of his own patients (with sickle cell disorder) that he'd like me to see. 'We've all tried and failed with her, but I think she may benefit from the type of work you offer'.

He explained about her case in detail. I was under no illusion as to the complexity of her case.

He said, 'I don't expect anything can help her now, so it's as if I'm asking you to take on the hardest case in legal history, and it's as if you're a newly qualified lawyer'. He paused briefly and continued. 'My point is, we won't be surprised if what you offer doesn't help her – her case is advanced, it's complex, and she recently nearly died in intensive care, but we feel we should give her the opportunity to receive what you offer'.

Later that day I went to see her, and she was happy to receive a treatment. She even shared in that first session that during her time in intensive care, she had crossed a river, and when she got to the other side, she found her father waiting for her. She told me he'd said to her, 'Go back, it's not your time yet'. She said she was happy to have had this experience and knew that when the time was right, he'd be there waiting for her. It was a very touching moment to have this conversation with her, and I felt honoured that she shared it with me.

The next morning she was due to be sent home, but the severity of her condition meant she'd usually be back in hospital as an emergency within two weeks. This was her life with this horrific illness, which many call a life sentence of an illness. I asked if she could come back and see me so we could continue in one of the outpatient clinics, and she agreed. The next week, she turned up for her appointment, and the following week, and for four consecutive weeks.

She didn't come back to hospital as a patient, as had been anticipated. In fact, one of my colleagues from the ward saw her in the local town centre a few weeks later and she was shopping. My colleague said she was looking radiant and smiling broadly as she came towards her, and through a broad, joyous smile, she said, 'I feel absolutely amazing'. They warmly embraced before she continued. 'You must please thank Suzie for me. She made a sweeping movement, as if pointing to her whole body. 'She's given me my life back!'

I hadn't done much. It was simply that something triggered in the action of the bioenergy or the relaxation and visualisation techniques, whatever it was, something activated her mind and body so that a reconnection could take place. It had brought her to a new realisation that she had a life to live, and tools that helped her be self-empowered to help keep her pain at bay, so that for as long as she had left, she was determined; she was going to live her life.

Shortly after I first saw this patient, Dr Bevan came to find me on the ward. He said, 'I don't know what you do exactly, Suzie, but I can see it helps and there's an ethical reason why we need to do all we can to help these patients. I'll do all I can to support you, in whatever way I can. We need this here. For them'.

It was actually because of my early patients with sickle cell disorder and leukaemia and seeing the ward lists of very sick children that the seeds of an idea to set up my project as a charity were sown. It didn't have a name, but from the moment I spoke with Dr Bevan and saw his patients, I was convinced that the project I had in mind needed to be wider than for cancer patients only, even though I was based on a ward which predominantly was treating blood cancer patients. I saw the need was much wider and encompassed very sick patients, from infants to adults. I realised I had a bigger job ahead of me than I'd ever imagined.

CHAPTER 15

Garlic Soup for the Body and Soul

Let food be thy medicine, and medicine be thy food.
—Hippocrates.

The doctors explained to me that I had bacterial meningitis. This type of infection causes inflammation of the membranes lining the spinal cord and brain, known as the meninges. If meningitis is caused by a virus, it will certainly make you feel pretty ill, but thankfully, it is rarely fatal – typically in around 1 per cent of cases. However, in the case of bacterial meningitis, even when treated as an emergency as early as possible to the onset of symptoms and crucially targeted with the right antibiotics, the mortality rate is up to 40 per cent. If left untreated, bacterial meningitis is always fatal.

I now had three lines of antibiotics flowing into my veins through an intravenous drip. I was effectively in a race against time and needing a large dose of hope that they would get on top of the catastrophic infection rampaging unchecked through my brain and spinal cord. I knew my chances of survival were slim. I also knew my chances of surviving intact both mentally and physically – that is, without amputation or brain damage – were fading too.

I looked up at the tall, slender pole with its curlicue end attached to which hung benignly a bag of liquid containing my last army: my antibiotics. I suddenly remembered reading a case study in a paediatric cancer journal of a young boy who had used the imagery of Pac-Man, the original arcade game from the 1980s, to imagine his chemotherapy as his own sunshine yellow army of Pac-Men, busily and enthusiastically gobbling up all the enemy cancer cells throughout his body.

I thought about him now. In the face of this mounting catastrophe raging uncontrollably inside me, I resolved to focus on the rhythmic drip-drip of the antibiotics and began imagining it being marched into my veins. I conveyed a silent wish to my body and to my embattled brain in particular, to please try to welcome them in and help them. Maybe, I suggested helpfully to my body, it could show my little antibiotic army where to go to find the bad guys, and maybe they could get little torches and point them like searchlights into all the areas of my brain and spine where the infection was hiding. I busied myself with this imagery. It was a life-and-death game. Each imagined scenario gave me the chance to factor in even more ways to search and destroy the enemy bacteria.

I was acutely aware how precarious my situation was now. I thought how I wished I had given even more thought to my nutrition before now. I had at least changed my diet and dropped the fizzy drinks and convenience-type foods, which had been my thoughtless staple whilst I had my gallery. A natural reclaiming seemed to be going on in my body, after I had my first bioenergy sessions. That was unexpected and certainly surprised me, in effect waking me up a bit to what my body craved and needed – and to my surprise, it was not sugar but vegetables and salad leaves! I confess, after that I didn't think in any more detail about it, and I certainly didn't think about going into the topic of nutrition in any detail. I added a few more vegetables here, cut down on the obvious no-nos there, and at that time in my life, that was about all I had in my toolbox of understanding.

As I peered up at my antibiotic bag, which reassuringly was resolutely engaged in its solitary task of delivering its contents into my veins, I understood this was the only hope I had left. With a sudden dismay, I realised I hadn't prepared the ground within my body by giving it the right nutrition for so many years in my adult life; only relatively recently had it been given the opportunity to tap me on the shoulder and get me to seek out fresh sustenance. The rising dawn of realisation now reached into every part of my consciousness, and all that stood between me and the edge of the precipice were the contents of that small bag.

The only active thing I could do now was to draw on a range of techniques I had already learnt in my bioenergy training and chi kung meditations: to try to stay calm, to stay present, and to not put any other burden on my already-overwhelmed brain. I knew this would help, so I made this the one thing I could do now. I had to park my fears that there was a fairly major chink in my armour: my lack of nutritional perspective. I had a reasonably large nagging doubt that I'd missed an obvious area, but it was too late for using up my dwindling energy thinking any more about that. Instead, I resolved that I would make changes to my nutrition – if – and it was a big if, I was ever to get out.

Around this time, there was a knock on the door. It was my good friend Anne. She had just popped in on her way into work to kindly deliver a little something for me. She presented me with a tub of homemade soup! Not only is Anne an excellent cook, but I was very touched by her thoughtfulness. She probably knew I thought about how generally unappetising and unhealthy hospital food can be! Actually, her idea was not solely about giving her friend something heartening to eat and look forward to (which it definitely did, especially when I had a gaping hole where anything positive should be) but her idea in making me soup had a different, more profound motivation.

With a broad smile on her face, she presented it to me with a sense of pride, saying, 'I've made you garlic soup!' She added, 'Lots of raw garlic, probably about four bulbs have gone into it!'

Wow, I thought, *poor nurses and doctors!* What Anne knew better than I did at the time was that garlic contains some powerful healing properties. Many of the major ancient civilisations, including the Romans, Greeks, and before them the Egyptians and Chinese predominantly used garlic for its medicinal and health-inducing properties. In fact, contemporary science has confirmed some of the beneficial effects of the humble garlic and that, contained within them are various sulphur compounds which are formed when garlic is chopped, chewed, or crushed. When entering the body from the digestive tract and traveling throughout the body, it delivers potent biological effects. This little soup, containing a powerpack of health benefits, was welcomed into my body with each and every grateful sip.

Now all I could do was draw on all I could to stay focused and as relaxed as I physically and mentally was able to. I knew this would help prepare the ground for the antibiotics to do their job, and give me the best chance of making it not only out of hospital alive but in one piece.

CHAPTER 16

(Not Always) Healing Sounds: Part 2

Minutes seemed to drag like hours; hours felt like days. None more so than after a lumbar puncture – because of the risk of increasing the pressure in my head if I moved it, I was told I had to lie perfectly still for six hours. With nothing to do and no means to occupy my mind or escape from the relentless pain, all I could do was watch the clock. At one point I thought, *Oh God, I wish time would fly.* To my astonishment, the clock suddenly dropped off the wall! I remember thinking right there and then that I'd better be careful what I wished for! I resolved to think about having a house in France and an Aston Martin – no idea where that came from, but that was my thought and I had nothing else to do but try to distract myself from the pain and enjoy a moment's freedom of thought before another hallucination took centre stage.

The pain in my head caused by the meningitis had now reached a skull-splitting pitch, where it felt as if my head would break open. I have never experienced a pain like it, and no amount of medication seemed to dent it in any way. It was as if it was being slowly crushed under the weight of a heavy object, which made my face numb. It started to make me wonder how long I could hold on through the screaming pain before I passed out. It felt as if the bones in my skull would split apart and shatter like a walnut in a vice.

To compound my misery, I was experiencing increasing hallucinations which rolled image after image through my mind. These had been running, like some wacky 3D movie since the day before I came into Accident and Emergency, but I had noticed that they had increased in complexity. Whereas before they had been every now and then, now they had become pervasive, occupying it seemed all the space and oxygen in my brain. Whenever my eyes were open, every thought became a complex movie, so that I now was becoming increasingly exhausted to even try to think as each thought was knocked out of my grasp by the hallucinations which took over and expanded on each thought. In my lighter moments I would call them my "in-head entertainment system", which seemed to amuse my doctor when he came to check up on me. He often enquired what was happening in the in-head entertainment system today and seemed genuinely intrigued at the detail with which I was able to describe each unfolding Technicolour scene. I couldn't avoid the hallucinations as they left no space for any other thoughts; instead, they seemed to have a life of their own and smashed over my newly formed thoughts as if driven by tank gears locked on to some unseen distant target. I kept trying to find a way to dampen their influence over my mind, but despite my efforts, my mental energy was fading as my mind was slowly being bludgeoned into a state of utter exhaustion.

In this unknown territory, I started to fear that my hallucinations were a sign of my condition deteriorating. My doctor told me the pressure in my head literally squeezes the brain and causes these hallucinations. He had just received the results of the MRI of my brain, which confirmed that there was significant swelling of the lining of the brain.

A short while after, I had a visit from the ward doctor. She sat on a stool by the side of my bed. She said it was "absolutely vital" that I did not move my head or put it under any strain or pressure at all. She made it clear that I was in a perilous position, and that it was just a waiting game. They were waiting to see how my body responded to the antibiotics. She was unequivocal in her message; brain damage was a very big risk for me now. Her words also stressed the urgency so that I was fully aware of the danger I was in and that I knew that I mustn't move or do anything at all that might risk exacerbating my condition.

Macarena

At some point around that time, I became aware of what I thought was the patient in the next room which, as my bed was positioned, was behind my head. He or she was incessantly playing one song. I had some empathy with whoever it was on the other side of the wall. I knew anyone on this ward was there for a very serious reason, so I told myself that maybe it was helpful for him or her to play it on repeat. Maybe, I reasoned, it was helping the patient focus on a happy memory.

I tried to be patient. I could do nothing but lie there motionless, trying to keep my thoughts buttoned up to avoid triggering a tsunami of hallucinations generated from one tiny thought. All I could do was watch the second hand slowly crawl up, then around, then down and then back up the clockface. Tick. Tock. Tick. Tock. As the minutes wore on and my eyes followed the slow circle pushing the minute hand on, my highlight was to see the hour hand move. I set targets for it to reach the quarter hour. Tick. Tock. My life passed this way for what seemed like hours, focusing only on my target of quarter of an hour at a time.

To my increasing annoyance, the song next door didn't abate. It began to really irritate me, so the next time one of the nurses came in, I said as politely as I could, 'Do you think you could ask the person in the next room to stop playing that song or at least turn it down?'

The nurse stared at me for a second and then said, 'I can't hear any song'.

I was surprised, and I said, 'Really? You can't hear "The Macarena"? It's been playing for hours in the next room'. I pointed behind me to the wall directly behind my head.

She paused for a moment, clearly deliberating as to what to say, before carefully choosing her words. She softly, almost apologetically, added, 'There's no song playing in the room next door, as there's no one in that room behind you'. She paused and gently held my right hand before adding, 'Just try to rest now, if you can'.

She must have told one of the doctors, as he came in and explained that sometimes the pressure in the brain can cause various unusual symptoms, because of the way the brain is swollen by the infection and squeezed within the hard, pretty immovable casing of the skull. He said my hallucinations, and now, most probably the tune, were part of this.

All I could do was stay calm and hope the antibiotics would bring the inflammation down. What wasn't said at the time, but what my doctor had said previously was that while my brain was expanding, this was where the real risk of brain damage lay. I knew what I had to do, so I went back to the tick-tock to the loud, incessant strains of the 1996 hit dance song "Macarena". I never liked that song before, so I have absolutely no idea why that was the one that popped up in my in-head entertainment system. It clearly had a malfunctioning jukebox as well now. If it had been something I liked I might have listened more happily in those dragging minutes, hours, and days, but oh no! To make my life that little bit more unbearable – it was just the chorus … repeated! Each line ending with a tuneful, ever so jolly but truly maddening chorus, "Hey, Macarena!" before starting the chorus all over again, "Hey, Macarena!" Again. And again.

Kakadu

My veins had collapsed, and my doctor had been trying in vain for what seemed to me to be an eternity to find one in my right hand or arm. He had given up on my left-hand side after that had failed to yield up any hope. The more he applied the tourniquet to my upper arm and forced a tiny and brave vein to pop up, the moment he tapped it and pierced my skin, it disappeared like a frightened rabbit down a hole. As this went on, I realised I was becoming increasingly needle phobic. I know it's a little thing in the scheme of the much larger issues and pain I was contending with, but I was getting so distressed, aided in no insignificant way by lack of sleep. I very much liked my doctor, Joe, and I knew he was doing the very best he could for me, so I didn't want to let on that I was finding this all a bit much. I bit my lip and focused on my left hand. I dug as hard as I could into the top of my index finger with my thumb nail to distract myself from the repeated needle stabs on my other hand.

At that moment there was a knock at the door, and my sister Karen came in, coat off and sleeves rolled up to the elbow, as was the infection control protocol on the ward. I was absolutely delighted to see her and my doctor, pleased for a distraction.

He looked up momentarily from his travails, happy to have a moment's respite, and without missing a beat, he said with a large grin on his face, 'Now can you please tell your veins, your sister's *are* the type of veins that I need? We both laughed.

My poor sister must have been momentarily confused by what on earth we were laughing about as we both stared enviously at the back of her left hand. Under normal circumstances she was entering with normally visible veins. Whether veins are visible or not, on me or anyone else, is not something I had ever thought about before. However, that day, my doctor and I envied her veins for all the tea in China!

Karen had heard about my "stuck jukebox" problems and how I was being driven demented by "The Macarena", so that cold winter's morning she decided to drive to London from Oxfordshire where she lived to deliver me some distraction. It was perfect timing. She brought me an incredible gift.

She'd woken that morning with a feeling that she should bring me not only a CD player but particularly a CD by Australian composer Tony O'Connor. She had lived in Australia for about seven years and had heard Tony's music there. For some reason she had the thought to bring me his CD, called *Kakadu*.

Tony's compositions, I was to discover, were unlike anything I'd ever heard before. He sensitively interwove evocative and uplifting music with sounds of nature that he recorded throughout his native Queensland. As I lay deprived of light in my hospital bed, I was effortlessly transported to a far-off place through the interwoven sound of nature and calming music. It was a magical tonic for my mind and body. I remember I was at a bone marrow conference in Hamburg, Germany, hearing a presentation by an Irish contingent, and they brought in images taken from their patients' gardens so that haematology patients who have to endure long stretches of time in isolation rooms had something nice to look at. I can't remember the details, but it struck me that this was a really good idea at the time. Now I understand why.

As I lay there for days on end, unable to move, I longed for the sight and sound of nature. I have often thought that with a bit of ingenuity, a specific project could be set up to put cameras in any beautiful place in nature so that patients who are absolutely deprived of its contact, like haematology patients are when in their isolation rooms for weeks at a time and indeed like I was, can still feel connected to the natural world if they can.

A Wagtail Comes to Help

I remember a patient I was asked to see who had had a particularly rough time with her leukaemia. She was starting to withdraw from the world so much so that she couldn't bear to look out the window any more. She said she couldn't cope seeing the world going on from her hospital bed, as she knew she would never be well enough to get out again. To cope with how she saw the world now, she refused to open her blinds and consequently existed in her isolation room, in complete darkness.

I was asked to see her by the ward's psychiatric clinical nurse specialist, Chris, as her medical team were becoming increasingly concerned about her. I had an excellent working relationship with Chris, who understood the benefit and would regularly refer me to see his patients as an additional way of supporting them at a time of great trauma and distress. I am sure I was really seen by him, to begin with, as a last resort, when no mainstream intervention was helping, particularly with some of his patients' acute anxieties before they went to intensive care or before bone marrow transplant. (Numerous studies show that stress and anxiety impact recovery, including wound healing, so it made sense to him and me to mobilise resources to try to bring down the anxiety levels of those patients who were by the time I was referred often exhibiting high states of distress or hopelessness.)

The lady he referred me to see was willing to work with me, and she gravitated strongly to visualisations of nature and healing sounds. She noticed the more I guided her through these nature-based sessions, the better she said she felt. Her room was one of the isolation transplant rooms which had a glass window between her room, a corridor, and the nurses' station, so it was easy to see that a change had happened as her window blind out to the world was now open!

I went to have a chat with her, and she said she just felt she wanted to look out now. She said she had spotted a wagtail on the roof below and that he came every day to the same area. It gave her something outside herself to focus on. She successfully completed all her treatment, and about two years later I bumped into her in the hospital.

She gave me a big hug and said, 'Thank you for reconnecting me with nature. I'll never forget that little bird. He was the highlight of my day, and I looked forward to seeing him during that horrible time'.

My sister bringing me in the *Kakadu* CD was a stroke of genius on three levels. One, it created a very welcome and different sound distraction to the intrusive strains of "The Macarena". I realised on listening to *Kakadu* that it managed to instantly block out the maddening repetition of that song. A result by any measure!

The second stroke of genius was that Tony O'Connor wrote his music to be at a specific timbre that is known to slow the brain waves. In particular, Tony composed his instrumental music to align specifically with the rhythm of the resting heart rate (sixty to seventy beats per minute) with the purpose of aiding a state of relaxation.

The third bonus with Tony's work is that he would take his recording equipment into the lakes, shorelines, and forests near where he lived in the mountains behind the Sunshine Coast. For *Kakadu*, which I'd never heard before my sister brought it to me, he recorded sounds as diverse as an evening chorus of cicadas and rainforest birds in his native Queensland, to the searing sounds of thousands of migratory geese taking flight at dawn.

Being as I was deprived of light and unable to tolerate sound, I couldn't imagine anything as my head hurt too much, but through the gentle sounds of nature on my deprived senses, I was able to feel cushioned in a place of sanctuary. There was even a piece that felt effortlessly refreshing to my overheated, weary mind: the refreshing tattoo of rainfall on the earth.

Another song I played over and over again as it somehow made me feel optimistic were of the chattering sounds of thousands of geese on a flood plain, and then en masse they take off. Hearing it today, it still makes my spirit soar. Here in France, where I am writing this book, it is spring. I had the joy a few weeks ago of seeing skeins upon skeins of cranes, hundreds at a time in the skies above me, travelling north over France from their southern wintering sites to the cooler climates of northern Europe. I just marvelled at this extraordinary sight of nature in flow. Like a tuning fork, seeing sights like this in nature, however grand or tiny, be it the flocks of cranes flying north or a baby swallow taking its maiden flight haphazardly into a bush, unaware of the enormous flight that lies ahead for it a month or so later, to the little bee working tirelessly in the amethyst coloured rosemary blossom, whatever it is in nature, it brings me back to what is important in life for me: harmony and balance.

With nothing else to do with my time, I read each introduction in Kakadu's accompanying booklet, and one of the Aboriginal poems that really struck home to me is from the song "Gagudju Life Force". Composer Tony O'Connor (1961–2010) wrote, 'These words are the conviction of the Gagudju Aboriginal people of the Kakadu National Park region'.

Despite the immense pain of having any sound reverberating in my head, I found listening, albeit quietly, to *Kakadu* created a deep peacefulness within me. It felt intensely essential to me somehow, as if a frantic roller coaster came to a standstill and in its place, part of me, bit by bit, was replenished. I continued to listen to track after track – and I shamelessly found the repeat button, so it quietly played continuously for days and nights on end. Even though I still couldn't sleep, I found I was moved from my now familiar state, a mental cocktail of worry, despair, boredom, fear, and sleeplessness to an unexpected, nurturing place of calm.

CHAPTER 17

Following a Light

Every time I thought I might almost have nodded off into a brief
sleep, the hallucinations would make me feel that I was rolling
one way or worse, falling out of bed. Despite the hallucinatory madness
going on in my head, some hyper-alert part of my brain kept uppermost
my ward doctor's warning: 'Don't move'..

Certainly that warning would have included: 'Don't fall out of bed'.
I couldn't risk that and when one night my overstretched nurse couldn't
find cot sides to place into the sides of my bed to contain me from my
fear of falling out of bed, all I could do was stay awake and hang on to
the mattress, hoping I didn't fall asleep. After the fourth night of no
sleep, cot sides were found and fixed in position. There I was, like a big
baby in a big cot. I didn't care the slightest what it looked like; I have
never felt so safe and so glad to feel hemmed in!

Around this time, Catherine, one of the first nurses I'd met and
given a bioenergy treatment to, and who was now an experienced Reiki
practitioner, popped by to see how I was and to say hello. It was lovely
to see a familiar face and talk a little, even though it was painful to talk;
it was still so welcome to have a bit of a distraction from the relentless
pain in my head. I told her that despite everything I had tried, I simply
couldn't sleep.

She listened attentively, and after I finished, she gently asked if I
might like to have a Reiki treatment. I knew she had trained in Reiki,

but such had been my busy-ness, I had not thought to ask her for Reiki before. I immediately welcomed the opportunity. Frankly, I was desperate to have any help I could. I didn't think anything could possibly get rid of my headache, but I welcomed the chance to feel relaxed.

She carefully repositioned my bed, unclipping the breaks. She slid the bed forward and removed the metal headboard so she could stand behind me. Gently placing her hands over my forehead, I immediately felt the warmth of her hands, and it was soothing. She then moved her hands to the sides of my head, and it seemed to immediately take the pain away. I don't remember anything else because I fell into a deep sleep for a few welcome hours. It was the most welcome respite I could have wished for.

When I woke, my headache had returned and was again in a full-throttle rage; this was to be expected, of course. But I had a chink of hope as I had for the briefest of moments at last experienced being pain free, and this was the most welcome gift that I could have received at that time.

The next day, as I lay in my darkened room, I became aware of a bright golden thread of light that seemed to be coming from somewhere outside. It was a warm golden light, which didn't seem to antagonise my light sensitivity. It seemed to be focused at about the level of my heart. It was no more than a foot away from me and remained on my righthand side. I became aware that it had a source. I also became aware that I was able to follow it back to that source. This awareness came with a sense that I was invited, lovingly, to explore it if I wanted to. The moment I realised that I could follow and thought that I'd like to know where its source came from (I had no feelings of alarm or confusion in this experience, it somehow seemed the most natural thing in the world), I found I was travelling along the golden thread. It was as if I was literally flying along but just above it.

I followed the thread of light from my bedside, out of my darkened hospital room. It rapidly crossed the fringes of London, and I followed. As I did, I was aware that I was somehow speeding over the channel. In a fraction of a second, or so it seemed, I had crossed France, until the next thing I realised I was crossing Italy at its southern tip. I distinctly remember this as I was fascinated that I was crossing over the "heel" of Italy, not just any piece of land but with the height and perspective that I had, I recognised it as the boot of Italy and, in particular the heel!

From the heel of Italy I continued following the golden thread of light in the same south-easterly direction, and I could see that it now crossed a large expanse of water. I seemed to traverse the water in an instant, all the while staying close to and aware that I was tracking back to the golden thread's source. Suddenly I found, to my surprise, I was at a destination on land, in the Middle East, and just on the other side of the Mediterranean Sea.

As I travelled, I remained close to the golden thread to make sure I kept following it, but simultaneously, I had a perspective of the globe, as if I was looking at it from a different altitude. I was both close enough so I could sense the land beneath me but also I was flying at what felt like high speed across a land mass.. I seemed to know where I was, so I never felt disorientated. I knew precisely where I was when I crossed southeast of Italy, as I clearly remember and indeed hovered over the heel for a while. I could clearly see the distinctive heel shape, so that I am in no doubt at all as to the trajectory that I had been on to that point, and also the onwards trajectory to the other side of the Mediterranean Sea.

I still had no way of knowing exactly where the golden light was coming from. I continued in a fraction of a second to track it across the Mediterranean, and in an instant I knew it was coming from a destination just on the other side of the sea. As soon as I crossed the sea and reached that land beyond, it seemed apparent that all I was to know was that it came from there. At that point, I was back in my hospital bed. I thought about it. It was real, as real as this sort of thing can be. Of course, I reasoned it could equally have been a hallucination, that I can't be sure. But it seemed to have a different quality about it, it wasn't random and it arrived with a lovingness and an invitation if I wanted, to follow it. That seemed to be the intention of the message, to follow it. The golden light arrived unannounced and on seeing it I seemed to be impelled to know where it was coming from. To follow it seemed obvious, and my task in following it felt totally purposeful and not at all scary.

The following day Jean-Cyrille came to visit me, and he shared that a Dominican nun who was in Beirut, Lebanon and who he knew very well had told him after I had been admitted that she had asked for a Mass to be celebrated for me at the Carmelite Nun's Community Chapel in Beirut.

CHAPTER 18

Drifting Away

I knew all too well that my long lack of sleep was putting me at a severe disadvantage – or more precisely, was putting my chance of recovery at a disadvantage. I was by now mentally and physically exhausted. I was desperate to sleep, but I needed to find a way to break through the pain to make certain I could sleep. I didn't trust that sleep would last long enough to be of any benefit or crucially able to help me recover. I was caught in the twin grip of both soaring pain and, at the merest glimpse of opportunity, my hallucinations, like a startled rabid dog, woke up and wreaked renewed havoc in my brain.

Knowing I was in a race against time, I made a desperate attempt to try to sleep through this roller coaster. I changed my strategy, and on that Sunday night, I asked the nurses for the maximum amount of painkillers that I was allowed, in the sole hope that I would be rendered free of pain just long enough to fall asleep and stay asleep.

I was given my last dose around midnight, and the moment I did, I knew something was wrong. No sooner had I swallowed the tablets, my stomach seemed to go into spasm. My exhausted body suddenly and violently used all the force it could to eject the last two offending painkillers, but it seemed it was intent to remove anything I had eaten not just that evening, not just that day, but with a force that was so violent it seemed intent to remove anything I had ever eaten.

As my body remained in this uncontrollable, frenzied state for around half an hour, within those first moments I knew I was in trouble. My doctor's words had been my mantra for survival: 'Don't get up, don't sit up, don't do anything that would put pressure on your brain'.

As these words hung in my mind, any faint hope I had to overcome the odds stacked against me now tipped my chances over the edge. The pressure in my head took on a whole new and alarming dimension. Up to this point, I had thought I couldn't cope with any more pain, such was the enormity of it, but now seized by the uncontrollable violence of what was happening in my body, I was completely helpless. I was gripped by the certain knowledge that each wave as my body continued in its relentless, violent task, each kamikaze wave of involuntary ejection brought with it the final, most likely lethal blow to my diminishing hope of avoiding permanent brain damage. *This is it,* I thought. I knew this was the end.

Still in the grips of this episode I remember with each spasm, knowing that I was moving further and further away from any point of safety. I would have given up, curled in a ball, and bawled my eyes out if I could, but the spasmodic reactions in my body refused to relent. I was slowly and violently being extinguished. The level of pain and palpable pressure in my head was now at such an insane level, it was as if something was screaming inside my head. It got to such a pitch that I thought my head would be better if it were to break open. I wondered if this might be possible. I didn't care anymore. I just wanted this cruel nightmare to finish.

The doctor on call that night was rushed to my room from Accident and Emergency. I remember him being very calm. I recall he sat on the side of my bed and said, 'You poor thing, this is so terrible for you. You'll be all right. You'll be all right'. I noticed he kept gently repeating the words.

I knew the battle my body was going through was putting way too much pressure on my head for what he had said to be true. I knew I was in trouble. Of course, part of me knew he was lying; he couldn't possibly know I was going to be all right, but I didn't care. At that point in my life it was the best lie in the world, because I clung to his words. It's odd how I intentionally clung to his words. They were as close as I could get to any hope in that hopeless scenario. Right then, right there, he gave me something to grab on to.

For more than half an hour I could not stop vomiting or retching. The force of the body in full-on ejection mode at times like this is enormous. I knew that each time my body went into a violent spasm, the resulting force in my head would cause more catastrophic damage.

I'm not sure if it was humour or desperation, but in the middle of what felt like a nightmare scenario, I said to him, 'I can't take any more of this pain, please shoot me!'

He calmly reassured me that he'd given me a fast-acting anti-sickness injection and that would start to work very soon.

I recall saying plaintively, 'You know, I'd still prefer to be shot'. I was only half joking.

Without missing a beat, his reply came back: 'Well ...' he said slowly.

I squinted up to look at him, and he had a smile on his face. 'We'll go my way first, but if that doesn't work, we'll discuss your option. Is that OK? How's that for a plan?'

I had to laugh. *This,* I remember thinking through my fear and misery, *is the very essence of humanity in action.* I was grateful in some odd way, despite it all, to have experienced such a wonderful exchange. His compassion, humour, and professionalism all perfectly measured to give me hope, keep me feeling as if I'm human and being cared for, and crucially then, doing whatever he could to keep me alive. I knew I was lucky to have a special soul in the right job looking after me that night.

I knew what was happening to me was placing me well past the safety zone. Thankfully, my body started to relax as the anti-emetics began to take effect, but now I was faced with a new problem. I became aware that everything I looked at had changed. Suddenly, the walls of my room, which up to that point had been an insignificant white painted cube, had transformed before my eyes. The right angles, created where usually vertical and horizontal surfaces meet at the top of the walls, and the ceiling, no longer existed. The neat ninety-degree angles were a solid, deep curve as deep as you see in an underground wine cellar in France or Italy.

I blinked, hoping that would reset what I was looking at. I expected them at least to recede. *Surely,* I thought, *this is just my imagination.* But no, they were absolutely there and as real as the walls themselves, to which they seemed to now belong.

I blinked repeatedly, hoping to shift these strange images around me now.. But no, each time I reopened my eyes they were there, unchanged with each blink, depressingly there, and as real as the walls themselves. *Oh no,* I thought, *how can they be real! What is happening to me?*

Keeping calm was my only buffer to push back the inevitable, but this was becoming increasingly difficult. I continued for a while to blink hard and hope some reset button in my head would make contact with my eyes and tell them to behave. Instead of resetting, the projected images accelerated. Firstly, I realised the room and everything in it was now coloured in a sharp, bright neon-green light. I noticed the colour, and what then came into view were intricate hieroglyphic patterns which covered all the surfaces in my room, including the ceiling. The room around me and everything I looked at was as if I was in a neon-green Egyptian burial chamber. Everywhere I looked, whether it was on the surface of the walls, the expanse of off-white window blind to my right, the small sink in the corner of my room, or the small clock which sat on the wall directly opposite to where I lay, every surface I looked at was neon green and covered in what I can only estimate to have been thousands of Egyptian hieroglyphs. There were rows upon rows of them.

The door opened slightly, and Bobby, my nurse that night, came in. She quietly entered my room, careful not to let too much light into my eyes from the dimmed, night-time corridor light of the ward just beyond my room. I saw the door open, but oddly, this didn't change the new room shape, its new colour, or its new wall covering of multiple rows of Egyptian drawings.

Bobby closed the door and came to my righthand side to check on me. I looked at her and could see that her face and uniform were now covered in neon green and intricate hieroglyphic patterns. I stared at her face as the hieroglyphs appeared to somehow be projected over the bridge of her nose and contours of her face, as if she was in front of a projected image at the cinema. I talked her through what I was seeing, so detailed were they that I was able to give her a running commentary.

I then heard her say, 'You're quite a character, aren't you?', but although I had definitely heard her voice, I realised something quite odd happened – when she spoke, her lips didn't move at all. I could hear what she was thinking.

For some moments I was fascinated by the intricacy of the patterns and shapes before me and all around me. A few years earlier I visited Luxor and had been inside Tutankhamun's tomb. What I was looking at looked like just that. I was now in what seemed to be an ancient Egyptian burial chamber. The only difference between Tutankhamun's tomb and mine it seemed to me, was that mine was neon green – oh, and in Tooting, London.

I was definitely not laughing at the time; in fact, the moment I thought about what was really happening to me, my defence wall of calm suddenly shattered, and I was plunged headlong into the full realisation of this new nightmare world. Where on earth was my compass point now? More than that was the lurking, dark thought, *Is this what brain damage feels like?*

Yet I was acutely aware that my thoughts were still absolutely lucid. I thought, *My thoughts are clear! In my head I have clear rationality, yet simultaneously, what I am seeing can't possibly be real. Can it? What is this split in my conscious awareness? How can I still have cogent thought processes yet be trapped in an "other" reality too?*

I pleaded silently with a Higher Power to help me. As I stared with incredulity at this heavily curved, hieroglyphic-laden, neon-green environment, I wondered if this was how I was going to spend the rest of my life – if, that was, I was able to survive this. I couldn't match up my new environment to any reality that I recognised; instead, everything I had understood up to this point about reality was now firmly upended. It felt like I was on a small raft drifting out to sea, with the terrifying reality that I was in the process of being carried further and further away from the safety of the beach, now a speck of colour in the distance. Realising there was absolutely nothing I could do but hope and see what happened next, for probably about an hour I remained transfixed by the extraordinary and detailed imagery all around me. Every ten minutes or so, Bobby would check on me, but to her I'm sure I must have seemed like a raving lunatic, as I studied her face and jabbered on about how the hieroglyphs looked or was found staring at a blank wall and excitedly describing unfathomable images.

At one point that night on the wall in front of me, a large drawing of man appeared. It occupied most of the height of the wall. Suddenly I could see complex mathematical formulae which were superimposed on the places where the organs were located. It was as if the formula changed in response to certain stimuli and it is here, in the altering of the formula that illness exists. Sadly, I can't remember enough of the detail of this, but this is the essence of what I can recall.

I remember feeling Bobby's calming influence towards me that night. It was something that I found to be hugely reassuring. It was as if I felt her compassion for my situation, and throughout every interaction she remained constant and kind. She simply and purely emitted compassion. Her gentle kindness was such a welcome and stabilising influence on me that night. I increasingly felt drawn to her calm energy as my condition deteriorated and everything that I was seeing, hearing and experiencing was now totally out of control and unfamiliar. What I was now facing was – literally – confusing and terrifying.I remember dwelling on this and feeling so powerless, wondering how does this end. I knew that outwardly what I was saying was causing concern, although Bobby did a truly amazing job at keeping her demeanour on an even keel. I was looking for signs of panic in her I suppose, that would correlate with my own panic and confirm to me the worst.

But she never let her doubts reach the space between her and me. I will never forget her humanity and how I needed to cling to it. By her staying in a calm, caring space, she allowed me to have something constant to hold on to. By then it was all I had. I think we only really understand the importance of the energy of intention when we are at our most fragile or most vulnerable stage of our life. I remember sharing my experiences of this episode with a colleague who was a palliative care nurse, and she was shocked that so much lucidity was happening behind the appearance that suggests that that person is no longer there in the capacity that we can understand.

Slipping away

As her frequent visits continued through the night, I noticed, despite Bobby's valiant attempts, she was now looking increasingly sad for me.

Through my neon-green haze, a pervasive thought had taken root in my consciousness: *Irreparable damage must have been done.* Maybe, I thought, *I have actually gone mad.* Part of me remained lucid and fully aware, but another part was totally out of this world and clearly – from what I was looking at – out of my control. Every time Bobby came in to check on me, her calm demeanour increasingly revealed what she couldn't hide from me any longer. Her professional concern increasingly fuelled my suspicions; something *was* terribly wrong with me.

When I asked her, she said she didn't know what was happening, that I should try to sleep.

Strange, I thought, trying to deny for as long as I could before collapsing under the weight of the inevitable truth, *why does she look so sad for me now? What's happening to me?*

I asked her to call the doctor. Bobby came back and said she woke him up, but he said to tell me to try to sleep, there was nothing more they could do for me at the moment. I felt a seismic faltering within me. Have they given up on me? *Oh no, no, no! Please, please don't give up on me. I'm here. I'm here!* I wailed silently to myself. My distress levels rapidly spiralled upwards, caught by the up-draughts of my absolute desolation. I begged silently, no words coming out, no one was there. I begged to whoever could hear me, *Please help me, I can't do this on my own.*

Just as I was contending with these emotions, I suddenly became aware that my body had become heavy, so heavy that I could not move my fingers to press the emergency call button. I focused hard to try to move my arm, if my fingers wouldn't move, I'd try to pick up my arm and drop it on the emergency button lying on my left-hand side about three inches away. My arm wouldn't respond; it was like set concrete.

'Help!' I tried to shout but couldn't even move my lips. Frantically, in my mind I was trying to keep a hold of my sanity and ignore the hallucinations surrounding me in order to make sense of what was going on. I suddenly became aware that I was feeling very lightheaded. I was now feeling very ungrounded, as if I was a balloon. I then realised a part of me was floating upwards. I was drifting towards the ceiling.

Oh no, I thought. *Oh no, I know what this means. No. No. No!* I yelled at the top of my voice, silently. My mouth locked. *Don't panic,* I thought as I tried to reassure myself. *I know I'll be able to get myself grounded.*

I tried to bring myself with my mind back down to earth. Nothing happened. I just moved gently, further upwards. Gathering my thoughts again, and with all the force my mind could muster, I recalibrated my focus in another attempt to try to ground myself. Grounding was, after all, a visualisation I was extremely familiar with from my years of chi kung training. It wasn't technically difficult for me to do this visualisation, and I would expect to feel its effect immediately. I had practised it for years and had confidence in it to bring about a sense of stability.

It was simple. Imagine you are a tree. You take a moment to imagine the type of tree to connect with a sense of its stability, and then, with your mind you travel down through its roots into the earth, imagining the root system spreading out in all directions underneath you that in so doing gives a sense of the enormous support network that's in place to stop a tree from falling over.

That's the intention you are aiming to engender – one of calm strength derived from the tree and in tandem with that, the nourishing and anchoring network of roots beneath the tree that bring strength and stability. I was used to doing this whilst standing with my feet on the ground where the feeling would be a greater sense of connection to the earth through my feet within seconds. If I was ever in a situation that would cause me fear or drain me I would take a moment to practice this simple but effective grounding visualisation.

I was equally practiced at doing this visualisation sitting down or lying down – I had even practiced it numerous times at thirty-six thousand feet in an aircraft. The key, I knew from years of experience of practicing this, was simply the power of the intention of the mind. It could also be whatever tree you resonated with. For me it was almost always a large old oak tree; for some reason that is the tree I personally resonate with if I think of a strong tree. Aware that time and indeed my life were slipping further from me, I demanded myself to focus first on an oak tree. I imagined the biggest tree that I could, with an enormous circumference, so big it would need three people holding hands around it to form a perfect circle. I imagined its deeply ridged bark, dark brown, and a canopy of leaves overhead. So far so good.

I then moved my awareness down through the tree and to its roots. However, I suddenly shot quickly into the earth beneath the tree. Too quickly. I was travelling way too fast through the soil for this to be a visualisation that would do any good at anchoring me or, as was the purpose to bring my slowly ascending self back down. I tried to command the image to slow down. I knew for this to have a chance of working, I *had* to get the familiar grounded connection that comes with the right, focused practice.

Instead of obeying, my hallucinations took over again, and I was suddenly travelling through the soil at a rapid pace. Again I tried to intercept and instruct myself to slow down and to *focus*. I set my intention that I wanted to focus on the very deepest tips of the roots, thinking this must give me the greatest sense of being grounded. Then I shot down one of the roots until I came to the tiny hairs at the end of the root. Still I floated upwards. I persisted with my intention; I wanted to connect with the soil. Next I was travelling through the dark, damp soil, past little white stones which seemed to stand out against the dark soil. Still I drifted upwards

I tried again. Perhaps I wasn't concentrating enough. I summoned myself again: *Imagine I am a tree with roots.* This time my hallucinations simply took over, and now, not only was I in a room that resembled a green Egyptian burial chamber, my mind gave me perfect quality movie-like images of a tree's roots. As soon as I thought about the roots in the earth, I instantly travelled down them, through the earth, through the roots, right out to their capillaries.

I wailed to myself, silently, *I just want to be grounded!*

Nothing. Again I travelled down, past jagged stones buried in the dark soil. I travelled past tangled roots of other trees, or the tree I was imagining. I didn't know. *I don't need this much detail,* I cried. Suddenly and to my relief and surprise, I found I was able to snap myself out of that imagery by simply stopping thinking of grounding. But I continued floating further upwards.

My rationale was becoming overwhelmed by the enormity of what was happening, I felt increasingly that I couldn't hold myself together much longer, I was exhausted through lack of sleep, through searing head pain and now, I couldn't concentrate clearly. On top of this, I was alarmed that I couldn't move, and equally that I couldn't get that part of me that was being drawn upwards towards the ceiling to come back down to where I was, in my hospital bed. I felt my mental strength and resilience ebbing away. In whatever way I tried to get back into my body I realised with increasing dismay, it was utterly futile; I was powerless.

I tried again to summon the help from the nurses who I knew would be sitting quietly almost in shouting distance from me, but I couldn't open my mouth to speak, let alone shout. I moved my attention to the emergency buzzer again, but I still couldn't summon my arm to move. I then focused just on my hand – *perhaps it could slide across, it's so near,* I urged to myself. Nothing. *OK,* I thought, becoming more desperate, *maybe my index finger can reach the buzzer. Surely that will be possible?*

I summoned all my energy with the force I'd need to move a stationary car. Nothing. Not even the faintest movement was possible. I felt another chunk of hope erode and with it, taking the optimism I had left too.

I was still aware that another part of me was continuing to elevate upwards. I was aware that I was completely weightless. Realising that my body was unresponsive, I was again consumed with a determination to use the full power of my mind to force myself back into my body. Still nothing. I continued my slow, gravity-free glide upwards. I tried one more time. I thought of a big tree. I made myself think about its roots and how they were holding that tree secure in the soil. It was like watching a documentary of the detailed under-structure of a tree. I seemed to just observe from a close distance, the intricacies of a root network of the tree.

I became increasingly frantic and frustrated by having no control over what I was observing. Nothing I was doing was working. Instead, I watched helplessly as each tiny detail unfolded on the topic of a trees' roots. The "documentary" simply continued to run, to unfold, and to enthusiastically present me with new images and impressions of a tree's roots. One minute I was looking at circumferences of each of the roots, and for some reason comparing their different sizes, and the next I found I was looking at older roots compared with juvenile roots, seeing how they were sent out at various stages in the tree's life.

This was certainly something I'd never even thought about before, and I certainly didn't want to use my failing energy thinking about this now. My impudence at being forced to watch this exploded. Suddenly, in one final fit of hope, I threw all my mental energy at the task to get back to my body, incandescent with rage at my infuriating and incessant in-head documentary. I commanded myself to be grounded. With impulsion equal to the force of my demand, I now found the root documentary took over again, this time I shot deeper and further into the soil, to be shown a complex underground network where I tracked along different roots and observed, right down to an almost microscopic level, how their capillaries probed and pierced down and sideways through the soil searching for moisture.

I had a gnawing fear come upon me: *Oh my God, am I now heading towards hell?* I didn't understand. This was quickly followed by a sombre question: *Am I dying? Have I died?* There was now a pervasive humming sound in the room. *Is this what dying feels like?* I wondered.

I continued to slip upwards. I yelled silently. Nothing and no one stirred. The realisation hit me with the full force of a hurricane. This was it. I was terrified. I was confused. I was in a desperate rage now. *This is not happening!* I yelled at the top of my voice, silently in my head. *This is effing horrific!* The hallucinations of roots continued alongside the visual hallucination of the green burial chamber, alongside now a deep humming noise. I howled to myself, emphasising each word and syllable as if that might get understood. This—is—im-poss-i-ble.I continued slowly upwards.

I begged silently but with all my might: *Help me.* There seemed to be nothing or no one listening. I was being slowly submerged. Consumed. I howled but no sound came out. If I could have cried I would have bawled my eyes out, I would have picked something up and thrown it. I would have screamed out loud. I would have broken something. I would have torn down anything in my grasp. But nothing. I tried again to call for help. I still couldn't make a sound. I tried to reach my emergency buzzer again. My lifeless arm unwilling to respond. I became aware that that part of me that was floating upwards was now closer to the ceiling than to my body. I don't know how long I had been struggling, but it incrementally dawned on me that nothing I was doing was making the blindest bit of difference.

Up to that point, I had fought the thought that I couldn't do this and kept trying different ways. But the reality was clear; nothing was working. I was exhausted both from lack of sleep as well as what had been an enormous mental energy expense in trying to get grounded. It happened in slow, creeping steps. I was out of solutions. Doubt was starting to creep into the cracks of my desperately resistant mind. My confidence in my ability to get this back in order was vanishing. I was now in uncharted territory.

With my optimism extinguished, my resolve and my fight were left rudderless. I was suddenly aware that I was totally overwhelmed by what was happening. I felt an insolent exhaustion crawl over me and take control of every cell. It was as if the banks of lights that kept my body going were slowly and deliberately being switched off, batch by batch. As if someone or something else had control of the master panel. It seemed there was simply nothing I could do. I realised my last-ditch attempts had been no more than a raging torrent of water after the rains in a desert; I had merely managed to keep life going for a bit longer before the inevitable evaporation and extinction.

I was incredulous that it had come to this. I was petrified. What happened next? This slow, painful loosening of my resolve led to what? I felt that I stopped breathing, though I have no idea what was going on with my body, but that part of me that was lucid, that has remembered all of this as if it happened today, seemed to hold its breath. For a moment I was aware I was fully adrift. I was in every way suspended. The impossibility of what was happening to me, right here, right now, gnawed away at my lifeless body. It was silent in my darkened yet neon-green room. I stayed hovering somewhere near the ceiling. I was near the window, its blind permanently drawn down to keep me in a darkened state since I had been admitted there. I hovered. The humming was still loud all around me.

I felt I was beginning to lose my grip. I felt my resolve collapsing under an unseen weight of something bearing down on me. I was aware I had been trying to keep my head above the water, but now I knew I had exhausted all my options. I had used up all my energy. My hope, the only thing that kept me fighting, kept me trying, was gone too. I was being submerged, dragged under the waves more than a few times in this struggle. I knew I couldn't hold on anymore. In this silent and exhausted moment, I knew I had no way back.

My mental grasp was spent. My mind blunted by all the effort. I was beyond the physical pain, though doubtless that was there, I can't remember. I was riven with sadness at the point of leaving this life. I had put up such a fight but I was forced to admit I had nothing left and I knew too that I had no more cards left to play. I was beyond anger at the situation now. I was numb. Simply numb. I presumed because of what I was experiencing the damage was irreparable. The violence of what had been done to my already swollen brain earlier that night must have done its worst.

As I continued to hover, my awareness seemed to shift. I knew that without any doubt I was out of options. I had no avenues left to try to escape what now seemed inevitable. My fight had been extinguished. I realised there was nothing more that I could do to stop this situation, nowhere left for me to go, and nothing left for me to try. I had used every tool in my toolbox to live, but it was torn open, every tool had been tried, and they were strewn everywhere. My toolbox resembled an empty carcass.

With the realisation fully dawning on me, and with no energy left for emotion or effort, I knew I had no option left.

I let go.

CHAPTER 19

Letting Go

The moment that I let go, I didn't think. I couldn't think. I had no more energy left for anything as difficult as thinking. I simply had nothing left. I was utterly adrift and silenced. I was hovering, as if paused by an unseen remote control. I was erased of any mental ability or faculty whatsoever. I was simply held by some means, in a suspended vacuum of nothingness. Me, my life, my thoughts, my body, my hopes, my plans, my fears – everything I was, or had, or didn't have, or had tried to do, or not do, everything up to that point where I had frenetically done everything in my power to try to save myself, evaporated. I was silenced. My mind was no longer flailing about. I was suspended. Completely blank.

At this point, and only at this point, when certain stillness had taken over, did I become aware of something being offered down to me. It came on my righthand side and was like something being lowered down to me. This feeling made me think of it as a rope that had been lowered down from a boat, as if I was in the sea, drowning. Of course, I didn't feel that I was in water, but it is the closest analogy to explain the understanding I had. I simply and without questioning understood that this was a lifeline. What was certain to my newly silenced mind was that this was *definitely* a lifeline. It wasn't tangible; there was no image accompanying my understanding of it, but it was at the same time both clearly and very lovingly communicated to me – to some part of my consciousness that this *was* a lifeline being offered.

It didn't have any physicality at all, yet somehow it appeared in the moment that it was offered and was held there for me, to have a very real physical quality to it. It is extraordinarily difficult to put such an experience into words, but I definitely understood it was "something", as opposed to a thought or an imagined state, or another hallucination. I was able to discern that this was different. It had an expansive, patient, constant, and loving vibration that was received with no contradiction into my quiet awareness. To receive this clear understanding that there was something that I had the possibility of grasping on to was at first a surprise and then instantly compelling.

What accompanied this feeling of a lifeline so close surprised me. I understood what the message seemed to be delivering directly into my becalmed consciousness, and it arrived with a crystalline precision. The message was able to penetrate into the quietened parts of my mind, able to transcend the visible world, and was able to arrive as a clear package of knowing. Its gentle guiding energy resonated that this was from a higher source. It had the same light-filled loving kindness that I had experienced when I was a child being shown the silver birch trees. I felt safe even though I was in totally unknown territory now and believed that I must have died, or at least be in the process of crossing over. I recognised this extraordinarily loving energy, and I felt safe at last.

The lifeline that came was clear. It was simply The Lord's Prayer. This was a great surprise because although I was brought up in a Christian faith, because of my childhood vision, if I were to classify myself with any religion or philosophy, I would be more likely aligned with Buddhism. It was not that I shunned Christianity, as I resonated with many facets of it, but I felt naturally drawn to a type of belief that was beyond the abilities of labels. Because of this, what followed was even more unexpected.

Not only was the sense of the Lord's Prayer crystal clear, it was accompanied by a very real sense of something being lowered down to me and being held there for me to grab on to. I hesitated for a moment, more out of shock that something so clear had come out of the total mayhem that had happened. The message was dropped into my consciousness with the purest clarity, accompanied by a sense of light that was extraordinarily gentle. It was expansive care and love.

The sense of light was not a physical colour but a feeling that brought an energetic lightness which seemed to permeate the oppressive, dark atmosphere surrounding me. I was of course at this point still very much out of my body! So the heavy atmosphere around me was where my body was, whilst my consciousness sat like a balloon somewhere between my physical body and the corner of the ceiling. I knew instinctively I had to mentally grab this lifeline and to do it now.

I also understood that I *had* to cite the Lord's Prayer, and an understanding was made clear to me that I had to reach the amen. I also understood it was important to keep repeating the Lord's Prayer until reaching the amen. That was all I received. But my task was clear. I did not know if this was to help me live or help me cross over, but I didn't question which way it was going to help me, I just knew it would. The direction on from that, whether back into my body or onwards, seemed not to matter. I was past the point of questioning.

Then, with all the mental strength I could muster I scrabbled about in my dazed and under-fire brain for how to actually start the Lord's Prayer. *How does it start?* I thought. After a moment or two, part of my brain was able to whir and clank into action. To my relief I could remember how it started: Our Father, who art in heaven … like a tiny baby clinging to the finger of a parent, I clung to my task with a single-minded determination that whatever I did I must get to the amen and then start all over again..

My brain was only able to locate some of the words, but I understood it was important to keep focused, to keep trying, and, once I reached the amen, to keep repeating it. I managed to get some of the lines muddled up, and I'm sure at more than one point I was saying, 'Our chicken, who art in the henhouse', but my intention was to say it even if my poor, befuddled, and exhausted brain couldn't quite find the right lane, the right line, or the right words. It was all in the intention. And that was all I had left.

Throughout this particular episode, my concentration on the task at hand was razor sharp, which again was a great surprise given the total and life extinguishing exhaustion I had felt just a short while before. I remember a passing thought again occurring, questioning if this was part of the process of dying or, if I was being helped to live but that thought somehow was never strong enough to divert me from my task. There was no time to stop and ponder. There was no time to question what was happening, I just understood this was a life-line.

I remember suddenly feeling as if I was filled with childlike wonder, and that feeling was accompanied by an unfathomable expanse of optimism. It was a feeling of complete wonder and the most profound sense of love. I was elated to feel like this after struggling for so long, but I was still hovering in mid-air. I persevered with my task; my awareness remained on its target; I had to repeat it and get to the amen.

An extraordinary thing happened. Each time I reached the end of the Lord's Prayer and noticeably, when I reached the amen, I felt that that part of me which was up, away from me towards the ceiling, would slowly descend, back towards my lifeless body below. I was now located somewhere above my head and slightly behind it. I could see, with each amen, what looked like a heat haze being lowered very gently towards the length of my motionless body on the bed.

I watched it, transfixed. I wasn't scared; the feeling remained very strongly of optimism even though I was not sure what was happening. At this point, I became aware again of a faint but distinct humming sound all around me. I could now see heat haze like energy more clearly. It had become a large swirl of energy in the neon-green light, which was now pushing at my feet. I realised it was pushing to come up through my feet. I was not expecting that. Suddenly I was gripped with fear. What was this? Was this safe?

I wondered if this was part of the dying process. I was terrified to let something that I didn't understand gain entry to me. I had no reference point for this. How could I? No one to my knowledge has ever spoken about this before. How could they, as probably this is something that happens after we've died.

I couldn't move and I couldn't call for help. I was so alone and was absolutely petrified of what was happening. I did all I could to try to stop this swirling energy from entering my feet. It was absolutely insistent and wouldn't stop. It was in a swirling pattern, moving clockwise as I looked at it, pushing to enter through the soles of my feet. I was confused and the more it pushed, the more frantic with fear I became. What if it was something bad? I thought, desperate for it to stop.

Oh my God, I wailed to myself, *this is a new hell*. Eventually, I couldn't hold it back any longer, and with every fibre of my being – such as my being then was – I reluctantly had to give in. As soon as I gave in, the swirling energy started to flow up through my feet. It immediately filled my legs. I was still petrified at what was taking over my body. I felt it flowing up, and after a short while I quickly noticed with relief that it brought with it a feeling of life again. I somehow was becoming more and more connected to my body.

At some point I realised my mind was back in my body as I was no longer observing it from above and behind my head. As the energy continued to swirl and flow up, my body came back into life. I suddenly and at last could move my fingers and arms. I moved my feet and then my legs. The motion-sucking heaviness had now completely disappeared. I lifted my left arm and looked at my hand. I marvelled at this, because I could. I had tried so hard to reach the emergency buzzer, but now I didn't need it!

There was a point when the humming stopped, but the swirling energy continued for a little while longer. It all seemed to correspond to when I felt that I was "full" energetically. It was rather like a balloon when it is gently inflated. As soon as I could move, I called my fiancée, Jean-Cyrille. It must have been about four in the morning. I left a message on the answer phone describing what I was seeing and what I had just experienced.

As soon as the swirling energy stopped, the neon green and the Egyptian burial chamber of a room instantly snapped back to how it had been – a simple white room. I looked around without moving my head. Everything was back to normal. I felt an overwhelming relief flood over me. I felt a searing exhilaration. I was alive. I think.

Then a doubt – was this too just an hallucination? I just didn't think it was; it felt real. But what had just happened? I felt an overwhelming urge to sleep. I needed to sleep. I remember thinking, just before I fell asleep, *Wow. If that was just a mad hallucination, well OK, but if this was really the spiritual experience I think it was, if this truly was the universe or God's help, then I won't have a headache when I wake up.*

Of course, medically, scientifically, and physically, given the events of the last few hours, not to mention days I knew it would be impossible that these symptoms, and the associated damage, could possibly be gone by the morning. I suddenly felt overcome with a sweet and very welcome tiredness. I didn't resist it and immediately fell into a deep sleep.

Early in the morning I woke and slowly dared myself to move my head. To my complete surprise, I had no pain at all. *Well*, I thought, *maybe that's just lucky because of the position my head is in on the pillow.*

So I lifted my head, something I couldn't do before. To my complete surprise, there was still no pain. Smiling, I tested my challenge from the night before and gingerly sat up. No pain. I then really tested the impossible and stood up. Now this was totally impossible – I still had no pain! *Well, I'm standing up now*, I thought. *The final test is to walk into the ward corridor*, and although it was still early morning there were lights on, and this was something I could not tolerate before.

I pushed open my door. I thought it would feel heavy but I it didn't. I then walked into the corridor. Not only did I still have no pain in my head whatsoever, I felt extremely well and strong. I went outside my room for the first time to the bright lights of the corridor and to my utter amazement and absolute joy, the knife-like light sensitivity that had plagued me until that point had miraculously gone too!

Later that day, the ear, nose, and throat doctor wanted to see me. Clearly the events of the previous night hadn't been communicated to the day shift of nurses, or perhaps it was because I'd been seen out and about that everyone forgot what had happened the night before!

A porter came to collect me from my room. I must say I was feeling confident so I eased myself onto the wheelchair, feeling like a child let out of school early! I was ready to explore the world outside, even if in this case it was only a wheelchair ride to the other side of the hospital!

The porter gently draped a blanket over me. As he wheeled me into the lift just outside the ward, in light conversation he asked me, 'How are you feeling today?'

To my astonishment, without thinking about the response – usually something along the lines of 'I'm fine, thank you', I instead replied with a triumphant, 'I feel reborn!' I was a bit embarrassed at my unedited reply, but it was too late. I laughed and added, 'I've no idea why I said that but I've had a hell of a night and I'm glad to be alive!'

I couldn't help grinning from ear to ear at what I'd just said, and more than that, what had happened the night before and to have my answer from the universe. I was not only pain free, I was absolutely euphoric. I was alive!

CHAPTER 20

Reminiscing

The day before I was due to be discharged, Jean-Cyrille came into the hospital with a video recorder. He said he wanted to capture some of the things I was saying. The following is written verbatim about a few topics that felt important to me immediately after my near-death experience.

On Nature

When I was really ill, after the first night, Anne, my neighbour, was the first person who came to see me. And that was after I'd bargained with God to let me stay. But I didn't know what His answer was. I just knew He was listening. I asked (God) to let me come back to the Ruth Myles Unit, because I haven't finished what I wanted to do for the patients.

There were three patients that I'd said I'd come back and work with, and if I died, I was going to betray them. I said, 'If You're taking me, please give me a sign, and if You're sending me back, which is what I want, if I've got a choice in the matter, please help me because I know what I've got to go through is huge'.

At that moment I got this huge waterfall of peace and unconditional love. I didn't know what the answer was, but it didn't matter because I felt that God was listening to me. In the morning – I think it was morning; I actually don't know as the room was completely dark – there was a little knock on the door. I could only just open my eyes through the pain. It was my friend Anne, and she gave me a card called Garden Path in Spring. I looked at that (image); I actually didn't even have the energy to cry, but I was crying inside because I thought, *I don't even know if I'm going to see my garden ever again,* but a little part of me said, *You will see your garden,* and that meant everything to me that Anne brought me that card at that precise moment.

(The following is in the recording, spoken through tears.)

And I had a little flame in me that said, 'Keep going because you will see your garden; you will see the jasmine in the summer; you will smell the orange blossom flowers in spring; and you will plant your honeysuckle; and you will smell the jasmine; and you will sit there drinking lemonade and basking in the sunshine and looking at the blue sky; and the birds and nature, completely, completely symbiotic. And right now I don't want to know what's happening in the outside world. I know there are terrible things going on (it was the lead up to the second Gulf War). I know, I can tell from people's eyes, but I don't want to know, right now. Because in here, in my little room, my sanctuary God means God, and out there (pointing to the window), God means power and greed and killing, and I'm not ready to go back into the outside world and hear it. Tomorrow I come out of here, and I so don't want to know of the evil going on in the world right now. I'll be ready to fight it, but right now, in here, God means God.

On Humanity and Compassion in Hospital

What I'm saying about God meaning God in here, and yet out there He's lost in the noise – not to all of you, of course, but to many. Sadly. What I wanted to say is the nurses and the doctors here are totally, totally compassionate. It is unreal. This journey really for me has been the most painful, the most frightening experience in my life. But the doctors and nurses have extended such care. And you don't get that in the outside world. It's rush. It's push. It's 'let me have a seat on the tube before you'. Pushing. 'Let me get in front of you'. 'I've got to go first'. 'That red light doesn't mean me; I'm going to try to get across'.

This is an unnatural way to be. So in my funny little way, I've not been bored in the last ten days because I have been absolutely basking in love, really. I believed I was really important to (my clinicians). I hadn't expected to be important to them. I expected they'd close the door and go home and forget about me. It's normal, they shouldn't take me home as a worry. But my God, every moment they said, 'You will be all right', even though I knew at times they weren't sure, but I believed them because it kept me strong.

And there was one time I was really ill last Sunday, and I knew, I knew it was so dangerous for me to be this ill. And I was on my bed and just being so ill and out of the blue, like an angel, came my doctor. Officially he's called Dr Jarvis, but he's Joe. Anyway, he was holding me, stroking my back whilst I was being so, so terribly ill, and he said to me, 'You poor thing, this is so awful for you', which I thought was amazing to hear a sentence like that. He was being human; he wasn't in denial that this was really awful. And then he said, 'You will be all right'. He kept repeating that. And my body was going mental in wanting the painkillers out of me from two weeks ago, it felt like. It was not stopping. And the pressure in my head was at a bursting point. And I heard his words, 'You will be all right', and I believed his words. Because it's all I had. Bless him, he rushed up from A&E to see me. He said these important words to me and rushed back down to A&E to someone else who needed him. I swear he arrived like an angel because I didn't see him come in. I didn't see him go. He just was there when I needed him. Bless him for that.

On the subject of doctors, they all were amazing. You can't separate them; they are all truly angels in white coats, and I really do mean it. If any of them are hearing (reading) this, there are no words for how you've helped me. But one of the most amazing things to learn was about one of my doctors, who exudes calm, warmth, and compassion. I was nobody to him, I was a girl who had meningitis – noncontagious, in case any of you are worried! And I thought, *This man has an amazing way*, and Jean-Cyrille was sitting with me and he felt the same.

And the next day, when he came to put in another of these Venflon gauges – which are my complete nightmare 'cos my hands and arms have no veins left – he was trying to find a vein and my veins had collapsed, so it was a little hard. We had an amazing talk. It turns out he is a spiritual man, he has travelled to Africa, to Ghana, where he said the joy of God is present in every person and life has a different meaning. He's been to Africa, and he's come back here, and he's my doctor at this moment. I told him, 'Your patients are so lucky to have you'. I hope he heard it because I truly mean that.

The staff are amazing here. The staff here are treasures; they are unsung heroes.

*

As I waited to be discharged from hospital, I lay on my bed, looking at the simple white room. I recalled how different it had looked just a few days before. I thought about and was so grateful to all the wonderful people who had visited me: my family, my friends, my work colleagues, my doctors and nurses, who all gave of themselves and helped keep me afloat just long enough to allow me to reach a safe shore. I thought back to that fateful call to the ward; if that doctor had not been there I would have fallen asleep. It would have been too late, there is no doubt. I thought about the bargain I had made with the universe just ten days before, after I was admitted, and the experience of receiving an acknowledgement from the universe in the form of an exquisite, all-consuming waterfall of unconditional love. I recalled how this feeling kept coming and coming in waves through those early dark days, and gave me hope that I was being heard and was crucially part of something far bigger and more beautiful and benevolent than words can ever begin to convey.

As I lay there thinking about everything that had happened, I had a beautiful vision. It was of a small sailing boat. It was skimming fast across the sea. To the right was a huge gathering of storm clouds. This little boat was sailing fast and had escaped from under the threatening storm clouds. As it sped towards the left into clear-blue sky, towards a distant horizon, its mainsail full, its name came to me: *Full Circle*. In an instant of knowing, I recognised this was to be the name of my project; the one I had bargained with the universe to let me live to complete. I smiled.

At that moment there was a knock on the hospital room door. It was the ward sister, Marjorie. She had come in to give me a hug and say goodbye. She said she didn't know how I did it but the team didn't think I could survive.

Her parting words were, 'Whatever you do, Suzie, keep doing it'.

AFTERWORD

Neither God nor Buddha nor any other spiritual leader or
tradition guarantees or encourages a pain-free life. Spiritual
teaching encourages us to grow past and through the painful
experiences – each of which is a valuable spiritual lesson.
—Caroline Myss, Author of
Why People Don't Heal and How They Can

We talk of the process of illness and disease in almost warlike
terms: "invasive", or "a virus attacked", whilst we, the patient,
often slip in the use of words that seem to compound our sense of
powerlessness: 'I'm suffering from …' – or worse still, we own the
disease: "my lupus," "my cancer".

As a young child, I had a vision that showed me life from a different
perspective. The journey often brought me back to this message and
provided me with opportunities to reconnect to what is essential. Can
illness ever be viewed as a catalyst for change? In my view, absolutely
yes. It is easy to slip into a state of anger at our own mind or body for,
as we see it, letting us down.

During the course of my journey through two separate illnesses
I found, despite myself, sometimes, that something essential was
happening to bring me back to my core, which in turn brought me back
to my childhood experience of the benevolence available to us when we
connect with the Infinite. I became deeply fascinated how our mind
influences our body and, of course, vice versa.

Before I had meningitis, I felt strongly that the need for compassion
in hospital, which was so evident to me when I needed it most, is the

hallmark of what I wanted to achieve with my hospital project and the reason I made my original bargain with the universe to let me live.

I knew it was important to deliver people with compassionate characteristics like those that had supported me with such humanity when it was obvious that I was deteriorating and probably wouldn't last much longer. To my doctor who sat on my bed (a no-no) and held my back (a no-no) and told me I would be all right (a no-no – you don't want to give false hope!) and who made me laugh in the middle of my darkest hour; to the doctor who simply exuded compassion and shared with me about his travels to Africa. To Catherine – a busy nurse who took time out of her hectic work schedule to give me Reiki at my time of need so I could get a short respite of sleep. These are the attributes that we not only need when the chips are down but should be honoured, recognised, and protected at whatever cost.

In my view, illness holds within it the seed of opportunity, to reconnect not only to ourselves but to the Infinite. As my friend and founding patient ambassador of Full Circle Fund Therapies -the charitable organisation I went on to found - Eric Evans, once said, 'In the moment of something awful are the seeds for something wonderful. However, will you recognise what it is – and most importantly, what will you do about it?'

The essence of the care that I received was precisely the essence of care I wanted to deliver through my project which holds the name Full Circle. My aim was always to deliver to the hospital bedsides of people like me, who were often like me, so afraid of what was happening to them and to bring to them a calm, compassionate and safe pair of hands. The only difference was that my project was providing it through integrated therapies, like the reflexology, massage, bioenergy and Reiki that all brought about in me a sense of wholeness, that was needed to piece back together the shattered elements of my being. Through my journey I learnt that touch therapies and energy therapies can have a profound ability to help someone who is facing a life limiting condition to come back into their bodies and to reconnect. It can offer a vital glimpse that through the body and the breath you can feel a profound sense of connection to the Infinite, to a sense of peace that transcends anything that can be imagined possible. The therapies I was lucky to receive brought me back, when nothing else could, to a space in time of absolute stillness. The hospital team gave me hope through their compassion. They reminded me with each and every visit to my bedside of the transformational power of human compassion, my starting point – what it felt like to be well. By their presence, they helped reinforce my fading grip on what I needed to do to try to survive. Like the sun, when it pierces through low, rumbling, slate grey clouds, it brings by its very presence in the gloom an almost euphoric feeling and a relief too. *You will be all right* are the greatest words I've ever believed. To the embattled mind and spirit, to be brought back to a sense of stillness and through that stillness guided to hope, is a gift for which there is no price.

That human beings have the capacity to do this for another fragile, vulnerable, and broken soul is the gift that we humans possess. It is sad that we often have to be so ill to see the best in humanity. But it is there, going on all around in hospitals, day in, day out, night in, night out. If you want to see humanity and don't fancy the route I took, look to your neighbour, and from your heart, simply smile. Next time you're driving and someone wants to be let into the space just in front of you, stop a moment, connect with your heart, and let them in. What harm could it could do? When you're the one who is being let out into the road by another driver, thank them; gratitude transcends; it is felt, not just seen. When you see something beautiful in nature – a flower emerging in spring, or the migration of birds high in the sky, take a moment, if you can, to be grateful that you're seeing a miracle of life right before your eyes.

Four more words that can help change our vibration, and that I try to use when things are difficult are 'look for the good'. Also, look for the light, because doing so can help break the negative train of focus just long enough to let light in. Through the light, this is our connection to All That Is.

Many years later, when I was choosing plants for my garden in London, I came across a page of different types of trees. My eyes were drawn to a picture of the whitest trunked variety of silver birch trees, which to my absolute astonishment is known as the Himalayan silver birch. I wondered, how could the 6-year-old me have known about a mountain range thousands of miles away, the home of the pure white trunked silver birch tree?

My childhood lesson of the birch tree remains etched in my mind. For me, every time I see this tree, whether it has been positioned on a busy urban street, planted in someone's garden, or plonked in the middle of a busy roundabout, I feel a searing joy. For one moment in a hectic world, I remember to connect to where *all is Love*. This serene tree's presence always makes me pause and take a deep breath, to recalibrate my own compass to something that is wiser and more beautiful than I can ever imagine. Not that I ever needed any convincing about what had occurred all those years before when I was a child, but its significance and teaching comes again and again into greater focus, and especially now, as I look at my life from a different perspective, I see now it has brought me full circle.

Since the project started in January 2001 it has provided over 24,000 treatments to more than 5,000 children and adults with life-limiting conditions. It currently has award winning projects in two University hospitals in the United Kingdom, delivering its pioneering 'full circle' of care into some of the most complex areas in modern medicine.

A percentage of profits from each book sale will be donated to Full Circle's Research and Development projects so that the vital role of holistic care in medicine is more widely studied, and to allow the 'full circle' model of integrated care to reach many more life limited children and adults when they need it most too.

www.fullcirclefund.org.uk

Full Circle Fund Therapies is a Registered Charity No. 1162010. Registered Company No. 9554871 (England and Wales).

Printed in Great Britain
by Amazon